Foreword

　本書は、「文学概念」を 1 章につき 1 つ取[ ] ではな
く、その概念そのものから、その概念が出[ ]、さらにはしばしばそれに対す
る批判的な見方までを豊かな語り口で論じた John Sutherland 氏の *50
Literature Ideas You Really Need to Know* を底本としています。いずれの章も、
文学を読む際（ひいては様々な事象を眺める際）、その内容について踏み込んで考
えたり、角度を持って論じたりすることができるような武器を授けてくれる内容
だと思います。このような文章を読む際には、常に文脈を考え議論に沿って読む
ことが要求されるため、アカデミックな文章や専門的な文章を読む訓練になりま
す。豊富な注や「作家・（登場）人物・作品リスト」、「解説」はこうした「読み方」
に導いてくれるでしょう。

　また、本文の文脈内での語彙増強を目指した各種ボキャブラリー問題をはじめ、
内容理解を積極的にいま一度促し確かめる Comprehension Check、実際に「文
学概念」を能動的・実践的に使って、考える力の涵養を促す Active Learning for
Discussion など、英語力はもちろんのこと、読む力・考える力を鍛えられるよう
構成しました。

　そして、一番のねらいは本書をきっかけとして、実際の文学作品や文学批評作
品を手に取り楽しんでもらうことです。そのために各章に「読むならまずこの一冊」
というコーナーを設けました。本を読む楽しさを知ることが、人生を豊かにする
と確信しております。

編著者を代表して
宮本 文

凡例

Reading Passage の注釈内で「▶ 解説」としている場合には、114 ～ 43 頁：
APPENDIX の当該章の「解説」をご参照下さい。

Contents

CHAPTER 1

Mimesis

ミメーシス

©Viacheslav Lopatin Rome – School of Athens, Renaissance fresco by Raphael in Stanze di Raffaello, Vatican Museum, Italy. Aristotle and Plato among other philosophers in the center of the famous painting.

ミメーシスは「自然に向けて鏡を掲げること」と定義できる。この古代ギリシア語は、「ただのコピー」と軽蔑するような英訳「模倣 (imitation)」より好ましい。「表象 (representation)」という訳も適切ではない。ミメーシスにはそれよりも重い意味がある。「ミメーシスの概念は」と、Ｓ・ハリウェルは近著で語る。「西洋における表象芸術とその価値をめぐる探求の全歴史の中心にあるものだ」。まことに基本的であるとともにひどく掴みどころのないものでもあるのだ。

 Pre-reading Vocabulary Check

日本語の意味に合う英文になるよう、次の中から適切なものを選びなさい。必要に応じて形を変えなさい。

> anatomy・primary・defence・overstimulate・extreme・
> generate・condition・lure

1. その国は異様な状態にある。
The country is in an abnormal _____.

2. 彼の著した解剖学の本はいまだ大きな影響力を有している。
His book on _____ is still very influential.

3. そんな極端な事例を挙げないでくれ。
Don't bring up such an _____ case.

4. 祖母はその本は弟には刺激が強すぎるのではないかと心配しています。
My grandmother is afraid that the book would _____ my brother.

5. その暴君にとって戴冠式が一番重要な問題だった。
Coronation was the matter of _____ importance for the tyrant.

6. この古い椅子の魅力を説明しよう。
Let me explain the _____ of this old chair.

7. 彼はその捕虜を擁護すべくすばらしい演説を行った。
He made a brilliant speech in _____ of the prisoner.

8. この機械はこうやって発電します。
This is how this machine _____ electricity.

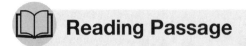

Reading Passage

1 The key to the literary door The problem mimesis raises is perennial, fascinating, and, finally, insoluble. Is literature 'true', or is it 'false'? It is, of course, both. Or neither – some would argue that the question itself is a 'category error*' (e.g. 'What is north of the North Pole?').

5 **2** The idea of 'mimesis' was put into literary-critical circulation by Aristotle, in his fragmentary treatise *The Poetics*. The title does not indicate an exclusive attention to poetry, but to all literary fabrication*. Aristotle was fascinated by the mysterious process by which certain black marks on a white surface or sounds in the ear become, for example, an 'epic' (*The*
10 *Odyssey*).

3 In his extended defence of mimesis as the way in which that trick is performed, Aristotle was quarrelling with an even more authoritative philosopher than himself. Notoriously, in his anatomy of the ideal state, *The Republic*, Plato exiled the poets. He admired the aesthetic* quality of their
15 'imitations' (they would, he decreed*, go into the wilderness outside the city gates 'garlanded*'), but their creations were intrinsically superficial, subjective and untrue. The critic Mark Edmundson puts it wittily*: 'Literary criticism in the West begins with the wish that literature disappears.'

4 For Plato, literature was the mere shadow of reality. Truth was the
20 province of the philosopher-king*, not the artist. Worse than that, poetry inspired emotional, not rational, responses. Mimesis created 'Beautiful Lies'. It led to bad decisions and bad living. Life requires cool heads and clear eyes.

5 Refuting Plato Aristotle refutes the primary Platonic objection (historical untruth) elegantly – turning the dagger against its wielder*.
25 Literary art (epic, tragedy, comedy, lyric), he points out, is unfettered by the accidents and randomness of mere history and can therefore, employing that literary freedom, articulate essential, eternal or higher truths.

6 For example: there never was a woman called Anna Karenina who committed adultery*, abandoned her family and killed herself at a railway
30 station. She is fiction. But the proposition with which Tolstoy's novel opens – 'Happy families are all alike; every unhappy family is unhappy in its own way' – has the status of what another novelist, in *her* opening sentence, called 'a truth universally acknowledged*'. Fiction, in this line of argument,

can be truer than fact. It can, in Graham Greene's phrase, get to 'the heart of the matter'*. Society needs literature's truths.   35

7 Aristotle's defence against Plato's second objection – that mimetic art and literature overstimulates the emotions (our eyes moisten at the death of Leonardo DiCaprio in *Titanic*, but we pass by, hard-eyed*, the beggar outside the cinema) – is less convincing. Aristotle concedes* that art does indeed move us: that is one of its primary reasons for existence. Athenian women, 40 he records, had been known to miscarry* and boys to faint when watching tragedy. But the emotion that literature generates, he goes on to argue, is 'cathartic'.

8 'Catharsis', like 'mimesis', is a word that does not yield* easily to translation. It can imply 'purge*', or 'laxative*'. Or, more relevantly here, a 45 medicinal *tempering* of the emotions. The lines from Milton's hyper-Aristotelian* verse drama, *Samson Agonistes*, are often quoted in this context: 'calm of mind, *all passion spent*'. Paradoxically (Aristotle loved paradoxes*), art works us up, but leaves us less, not more, emotional, and better able to make rational decisions. Plato, in other words, should welcome 50 literature as something that clears the mind.

9 The problem of the catharsis theory   It's an elegant riposte* but it has something of the sleight of hand* about it. A recurrent objection against the 'cathartic' line of defence is that it necessarily overvalues literature for its 'affective*' quality: how we respond to it. Taken to its logical extreme, 55 'catharsis' could be thought to imply that the art that moves us most must be the best literature. Which, on the basis of the teardrops it generates, would make some Mills and Boon* 'weepies*' better novels than *Pride and Prejudice*.

10 Controversy has raged* for centuries around Aristotle's theory of mimesis and what it means for literature and society. Plato, as has been said, booted 60 the poet out of the Republic; Aristotle wishes to keep him/her as an honoured citizen within the city walls. George Orwell, in his essay 'Inside the Whale', argued that exile is, ideally, where the writer should be. Society (particularly totalitarian* society) swallows up the domesticated writer, as Leviathan does Jonah. Better Solzhenitsyn, kicked into exile in 1973, than those hacks who 65 stayed as privileged members of the Soviet 'Writers' Union'*.

11 Strategically, Orwell argued, the place to be is outside the beast, harpoon in hand, not in its belly. James Joyce, with a more modernist* outlook*, believed the writer should create in a condition of 'silence, *exile*, and cunning'*.

⓬ The Marxist writer Bertolt Brecht founded his aesthetic on contradiction of Aristotle's mimesis and literature or drama that is so 'magnetically' real that we are sucked in and 'carried away'. We should sternly resist the lure of mimesis, Brecht insisted. It is the drug of literature. The quarrels go on, and will do as long as there is literature.

❶ **category error**：「カテゴリー錯誤」 ▶解説
❷ **fabrication**：「製作物」
❸ **aesthetic**：「美的な」
decree：「命じる」
garland：「花輪で飾る」
wittily：「機知に富んで」
❹ **the philosopher-king**：「哲人王」 ▶解説
❺ **wielder**：「使い手」
❻ **adultery**：「不義、不倫」
the status ... acknowledged：▶解説
'the heart of the matter'：「「事件の核心」」 ▶解説
❼ **hard-eyed**：「無慈悲な」
concede：「（譲歩して）認める」
miscarry：「流産する」
❽ **yield**：「従う」
purge：「浄化」
laxative：「下剤」
hyper-Aristotelian：「超アリストテレス的な」
paradox：「逆説、パラドクス」 正当な推論に拠りながら、一般には受け入れがたい結論に至る説。
❾ **riposte**：「反撃、しっぺ返し」
sleight of hand：「手先の早わざ」
affective：「情動の」
Mills and Boon：「ミルズ＆ブーン」 ▶解説
weepy：「お涙頂戴もの」
❿ **rage**：「盛んに起こる」
totalitarian：「全体主義の」
the Soviet 'Writers' Union'：「ソヴィエト連邦「作家同盟」」 ▶解説
⓫ **modernist**：「モダニストの」 ▶解説
outlook：「見地」
'silence, *exile*, and cunning'：「「沈黙、流浪、狡猾」」 ▶解説

Post-reading Vocabulary Check

➤ 日本語の意味に合う英文になるよう、次の中から適切な 動詞 を選び、必要に応じて形を変えなさい。

quarrel・employ・commit・acknowledge・exile・moisten・move・faint

1. 彼女はよろこびで気絶するところだった。
She almost _____ from joy.

2. 彼らはその石の所有をめぐって揉めた。
They _____ over who should own the stone.

3. この作家は悲しみを描くのに、ときどき独自の比喩を使う。
This writer sometimes _____ unique figures of speech to describe a sense of grief.

4. 国王は反逆者を追放した。
The king _____ the traitor.

5. 土の表面を湿らせるのを忘れないように。
Don't forget to _____ the surface of the soil.

6. 彼は今日、もっとも抒情的なピアニストの一人として認められている。
He is _____ as one of the most lyrical contemporary pianists.

7. 彼は自殺を試みた。
He tried to _____ suicide.

8. 彼女は僕のヴァイオリン演奏に大変感動したようだ。
My violin performance seems to have _____ her a lot.

➤ 下記の 形容詞または副詞 ＝英英・英日の語義が成立するように、空欄を埋めなさい。

1. e □□□□□□□ = only, single 「それだけに限られた、専用の」

2. a □□□□□□□□□□ = definitive 「権威ある」

3. intrinsically = es □□□□□□□□ 「固有に、本質的に」

4. s □□□□□□□□□ = cursory, thoughtless 「表面的な、浅薄な」

5. u □□□□□□□□ = unrestrained, free 「束縛されていない」

6. u □□□□□□□□□ = always, globally 「普遍的に」

7. convincing = p □□□□□□□□ 「説得力のある」

8. r □□□□□□□□ = pertinently 「関連して」

Comprehension Check **True or False**

下の英文が本文の内容として正しい場合は T、間違っている場合は F を選びましょう。

1. Plato was an ardent supporter of mimesis. (T / F)
2. Aristotle agreed with Plato that poets would have to be honored inside the city gates. (T / F)
3. Plato claims that mimesis would hurt people's rationality. (T / F)
4. 'Catharsis' might link Aristotle and Plato together in that it eventually calms down people's emotions. (T / F)
5. Tolstoy's *Anna Karenina* is a precise biography of a woman who lived in nineteenth century Russia. (T / F)

Comprehension Check **Multiple Choice**

本文の内容に照らして最も正しいものを a 〜 c の中から選んで○をつけなさい。

1. Which of the following does NOT apply to Plato's view toward literature?
   a. It is indispensable for literature to develop human beings' rationality.
   b. People can reach the truth without it.
   c. It may prevent people from making fair judgements.

2. Aristotle claims that literary work can express more universal truths than historical facts because
   a. it is free from contingency of what actually happens.
   b. more people would join in literary activity striving for the honor and the garland.
   c. he does not admit Plato as the philosopher-king.

3. *Samson Agonistes* shows
   a. how ardently Milton worshiped Plato.
   b. how 'catharsis' in literature works.
   c. how easily a verse drama becomes weepy.

4. Overvaluing the significance of 'catharsis' might be dangerous because
   a. it may lead us to a misapprehension that the more tears it generates, the better the book is.
   b. it may actually loosen people's bowels.
   c. some may notice that it is just a rhetorical sleight.

5. Solzhenitsyn was exiled because

    a. he kept insisting that he should be a member of the Soviet 'Writer's Union'.

    b. he criticized the totalitarianism of his country.

    c. he was a radical totalitarian.

 ACTIVE LEARNING for Discussion

1. 第 6 パラグラフに 'Fiction, in this line of argument, can be truer than fact' とあります。「フィクション（fiction）」が「事実（fact）」よりも「真実（true）」であるような具体例を、自身の実生活に即して考えてみましょう。

2. 第 8・9 パラグラフ「カタルシス」効果について、文学そして文学以外の芸術（音楽、映画、美術など）で、実際に体験したことがあるかどうか、ペアまたはグループで話し合ってみましょう。

3. 第 6 パラグラフ最終行「社会が文学の真実を求めている」とは具体的にどのようなことか、ペアまたはグループで話し合ってみましょう。

 読むならまずこの一冊

プラトン『国家』（岩波文庫など）
「洞窟の比喩」はもちろん、正義、芸術、教育、性差などをめぐって交わされる対話の数々は 2000 年以上の時を経て、いよいよみずみずしく私たちに迫ってくる。最終巻の 10 巻に現れるプラトンの詩人追放論についてもよく考えてみよう。

CHAPTER 2

曖昧さ

Ambiguity

「僕が言葉を使うときにはね」とハンプティ・ダンプティは言った。「その言葉は、僕がそう意味するように選んだようにちょうど意味するようになるんだよ。まさしく、ちょうどその意味にね」。「問題はね」とアリスは反論した。「あなたが言葉にそう意図したのと同じだけの違うことを意味させることができるかどうかね」アリスは女の子のなかでもっとも分別があり、もちろん正しい。しかし文学以上に言葉に様々な意味を様々な方法で持たせることができる所はどこにもない。言い換えれば、文学は最も高い次元まで引き上げられた曖昧さなのだ。その目的は、最も高尚なところでは、混乱させることではなく、物事と言語の単純化できない複雑さを捉えることにある。

 ## Pre-reading Vocabulary Check

日本語の意味に合う英文になるよう、次の中から適切なものを選びなさい。必要に応じて形を変えなさい。

> implementation・insult・enigma・brute・legitimacy・valour・
> reverence・criterion

1. 勇気の大切な部分は分別である。

The important part of _____ is discretion.

2. 謎めいたハムレットの性格が読者を惹きつけてきた。

The _____ of Hamlet's personality has fascinated readers.

3. 我々の製品は全ての安全基準を満たしている。

Our products fit every _____ of safety.

4. 大統領は公民権法の施行を推進した。

The President pushed forward with the _____ of the Civil Rights Act.

5. オセロは獣のような夫だった。

Othello was a _____ of a husband.

6. その侮辱はアフリカ系アメリカ人に向けられたものであった。

That _____ was directed at African Americans.

7. ハムレットは新国王に畏敬の念を抱かなかった。

Hamlet didn't feel _____ for the new king.

8. 彼の王位継承が正当なものか疑わしい。

The _____ of his succession to the throne is in question.

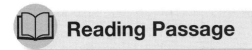

Reading Passage

🔊 Audio 1-03

1 **The inherent slipperiness* of literature**   Literature is, of its very nature, polyvalent* – it can mean different things at the same time. Historically it can also mean different things at different times (think of *Uncle Tom's Cabin* in 1864, during the Civil War*, and in 1964, on the implementation of the Civil Rights Act*, when the term 'Uncle Tom' had 5 become a deadly insult between African Americans). Biographically too, a work of literature can mean different things at different times of one's life. Jack Kerouac's 'Beat Bible*' *On the Road* is a different novel for me now than it was for the 17-year-old, romantically footloose, writer of this book.

2 This multi-meaningfulness operates from the level of whole text to the 10 single word. Take the work T. S. Eliot called the 'Mona Lisa* of Literature', Shakespeare's *Hamlet*. Every age interprets the play's enigmas differently, sometimes wildly so (is Hamlet mad, enquired Oscar Wilde; or merely the critics of *Hamlet*?). The nineteenth century saw the Prince of Denmark as a noble philosopher. Coleridge hazarded, proudly, that he had a 'smack* of 15 Hamlet' in himself. In the twentieth century, it's not unusual for Hamlet to be seen by feminist critics as a homicidal, sexually predatory brute, spouting stale truisms and obnoxious self-pity.

3 Has anyone, over the centuries, got *Hamlet* (or Hamlet) right, or has everyone? Can anyone? *Tot homines, quot sententiae**, the Latin proverb 20 says. There are as many opinions as there are people.

4 Does the view that Hamlet is a cross-dressed* woman (an interpretation that has been seriously advanced), or that he is gay, or that he is the victim of an unresolved Oedipus complex* have the same legitimacy as T. S. Eliot's sage deliberations* about the Mona Lisa of literature? 25

5 **Verbal ambiguity**   Moving down the scale, one can discover polyvalence at the micro-level of the simplest of words. Sticking with *Hamlet*, there is an early exchange between Claudius and his new stepson (whose father Claudius has murdered, although Hamlet does not yet know it) in which the King politely enquires why the dark clouds hang over him. Hamlet replies, 30 cuttingly: 'Not so, my Lord. I am too much i' the *sun*.' It's a homophonic pun*: son/sun. Puns ('puncepts*', as some modern commentators call them) embody 'ambiguity' in its most crystalline* form.

6 Ambiguity became the buzziest of buzzwords* in the 1930s, with William
Empson's monograph* *Seven Types of Ambiguity* (1930) leading the way. The
book was a version of the 22-year-old Empson's PhD thesis (it actually began
as a fortnightly undergraduate essay. He was very smart).

7 Of the multitude (many more than seven) of ambiguities Empson discerns,
consider a particularly brilliant example, from Gerard Manley Hopkins'
poem, 'The Windhover'. The bird (a falcon) closes its wings when it drops
down on its prey, falling like a stone. For Hopkins, the bird is a metaphor for
Christ, whose arms were extended like wings on the cross, and folded in the
tomb:

> 'Brute beauty and valour and act, oh, air, pride, plume, here
>
>   Buckle! AND the fire that breaks from thee* then, a billion
>
> Times told lovelier, more dangerous, O my chevalier*!'

'Buckle', Empson observed, here means two contrary things. One is 'girding',
pulling oneself together, as one *buckles* a belt, or *buckles* on armour. The
other is 'bend-to-breaking' – as in a *buckled* or crumpled bicycle wheel. Which
is it in 'The Windhover'? Both. Why? Because it's poetry.

8 **Psychoanalytic* ambiguities**   There was another exciting doctrine
abroad in the 1930s – psychoanalysis. One of the more daring suppositions
among ambiguity hunters (who liked to hang their big game* up on
imaginary walls, like so many trophies) was that there could be Freudian
ambiguities ('slips*', or what Freud called 'parapraxes*') in texts of which the
authors themselves were unconscious. Consider what Hamlet mutters to
himself before going into his climactic tête-à-tête* with his mother, in her
'closet' (bedchamber):

> 'O heart, lose not thy nature, let not ever
>
> The soul of Nero enter this firm bosom,
>
> Let me be cruel not unnatural.'

Nero, of course, is reported to have killed his mother, Agrippina. This is the
primary meaning. Other, more scurrilous* accounts record an incestuous*
relationship between the Emperor (when 'heated with wine') and his mother.
A bedroom scene is imminent. Has Hamlet resolved his Oedipal complex – or
is some awful 'unnatural' coupling* in prospect? It's hard to think that
Shakespeare means us to wonder, but does the text unconsciously prompt us
in that direction, implying what its author dare not?

9 Reverence for the irreducible* ambiguity of great literature was codified*

in a teaching technique labelled 'practical criticism*' in the UK, and 'new 70
criticism' in the US. Educationally it was immensely refreshing, sweeping
away the previously reigning orthodoxies of philology*. Practical criticism
placed the 'contextless' literary text in clinical isolation, where it could be
subjected to the scalpel-like* investigations of 'close reading*'.

10 But what was this endless hunt for meanings – lemon squeezing, the 75
Marxist critic* Terry Eagleton calls it – *for*? Young Empson likened* the
ambiguity virtuoso* to a conjuror* pulling rabbits out of a hat. Discovering
hitherto undiscovered ambiguities proved you were cleverer than other
readers.

11 But ultimately all this close reading by clever readers did, it was felt, go 80
somewhere important. It validated* the best texts, creating, as you went, a
canon – the curriculum of worthwhile literature. Ambiguity was the criterion.
The more pliant* literary texts were – the more lemon juice you could
squeeze out of them – the better they were. Some forms and ages of literature
lent themselves to* the close-reading method better than others: notably 'the 85
School of Donne*' and 'moderns' (like Hopkins). As Empson himself observed,
some historical periods – notably the Augustans* – were by nature
disambiguators*. Those periods became unfashionable in the decades when
practical criticism was riding high* – as, just at the moment, it no longer
does. 90

---

1 slipperiness：「つかみどころのなさ」
polyvalent：「多くの面を持つ」
the Civil War：「南北戦争（1861-65）」
the Civil Rights Act：「公民権法」1964年公民権法は米国の黒人差別撤廃を規定した代表的なもの。
Beat Bible：「ビート世代のバイブル」▶解説 Beat Generation
2 Mona Lisa：「モナリザ」レオナルド・ダ・ヴィンチ作の謎めいた微笑をたたえた女性の肖像画。
smack：「香り、…じみたところ」
クゥオト・ホミネース・トト・センテンティアエ
3 *Tot homines, quot sententiae*：「十人十色」
4 cross-dressed：「異性の服装をした」
Oedipus complex：「エディプス・コンプレックス」▶解説
deliberation：「（あらゆる面からの）審議」
5 homophonic pun：「同音異字の語呂合わせ」
puncept：「パンセプト」語呂合わせを意味する pun と concept を掛け合わせた造語。
crystalline：「明快な」
6 the buzziest of buzzwords：「流行した専門用語の中で最も口にのぼったもの」
monograph：「研究論文」
7 thee：「汝を」▶解説 thou
chevalier：「騎士」
8 psychoanalytic：「精神分析の」

game：「獲物」

slip：「言い間違い」

parapraxes（複）（parapraxis（単））：「錯誤行為」心理学用語

tête-à-tête：「対談」

scurrilous：「下世話な」

incestuous：「近親相姦の」

coupling：「まぐわい」

9 irreducible：「それ以上単純化できない」

codify：「体系化する」

practical criticism：「実践批評」▶解説

philology：「文献学」

scalpel：「外科用メス」

close reading：「精読」▶解説

10 the Marxist critic：「マルクス主義批評」▶ Chapter 7 Base/ Superstructure

liken：「なぞらえる」

virtuoso：「名手」

conjuror：「手品師」

11 validate：「認証する」

pliant：「柔軟な」

lend oneself to：「…に適している」

the School of Donne：「（ジョン・）ダン学派」一般的に 17 世紀の形而上詩人たちを指す

the Augustans：「英国 18 世紀前半オーガスタン時代（古典主義）の作家たち」▶解説 Augustan age

disambiguator：「曖昧さを排する傾向にあるもの」

ride high：「うまくいく」

Post-reading Vocabulary Check

➤ 日本語の意味に合う英文になるよう、次の中から適切な 動詞 を選び、必要に応じて形を変えなさい。

operate・hazard・reply・embody・crumple・resolve・imply・validate

1. 彼女は間違いを恐れずに言ってみた。
She ＿＿＿＿＿＿＿＿ a guess.

2. その問題はまだ未解決である。
That issue is still to be ＿＿＿＿＿＿＿＿.

3. 委員会は選挙の正当性を認めた。
The committee ＿＿＿＿＿＿＿＿ an election.

4. ジェフ・クーンズの立体彫刻は現代人のもつ欲望を具現化している。
Jeff Koons' sculptures ＿＿＿＿＿＿＿＿ the desires modern people have.

5. 工場はフル稼働している。
The factory ＿＿＿＿＿＿＿＿ at capacity.

6. ハムレットは、決心はついたと答えた。
Hamlet ＿＿＿＿＿＿＿ that his mind was made up.

7. 彼女は沈黙することによって同意をほのめかした。
Her silence ＿＿＿＿＿＿＿ agreement.

8. 彼は紙をくしゃくしゃにして丸めた。
He ＿＿＿＿＿＿＿＿ the paper into a ball.

➤ 下記の 形容詞または副詞 =英英・英日の語義が成立するように、空欄を埋めなさい。

1. n □□□□ =righteous, honourable 「気高い、立派な」

2. p □□□□ ly = contently, joyfully 「得意げに、誇らしげに」

3. h □□□□□□□ = murderous, violent 「殺人の、殺人を犯しそうな」

4. ob □□□□□□□ = disgusting, awful 「不愉快な、感じの悪い」

5. p □□□□□ ly = courteously, respectfully 「礼儀正しく」

6. fortnightly = once in t □□ weeks 「2 週間ごとに」

7. previously = f □□□□□ ly, earlier 「以前に」

8. reigning = p □□□□□□ ing, popular 「全盛の」

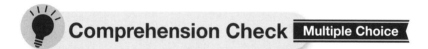

Comprehension Check — True or False

下の英文が本文の内容として正しい場合は T、間違っている場合は F を選びましょう。

1. *Uncle Tom's Cabin* has two different versions, in 1864 and 1964.　　　(T / F)
2. Some feminists regard Hamlet as a sexual abuser.　　　(T / F)
3. 'Son/sun' (l. 32) is a homographic pun.　　　(T / F)
4. Practical criticism puts an emphasis on historical contexts.　　　(T / F)
5. Practical criticism is no longer in fashion.　　　(T / F)

Comprehension Check — Multiple Choice

本文の内容に照らして最も正しいものを a ～ c の中から選んで○をつけなさい。

1. 'The inherent slipperiness of literature' (l. 1) means that
   a. it tends to make mistakes.
   b. its meaning is hard to determine.
   c. its meaning is easy to determine.

2. T. S. Eliot called Hamlet the 'Mona Lisa of Literature' (l. 11) because
   a. there were many different interpretations in every age.
   b. Hamlet always smiled mysteriously.
   c. Hamlet looked like Mona Lisa in appearance.

3. According to Empson, which of the following does NOT apply to the meanings of 'buckle' in 'the Windhover'?
   a. to pull oneself together
   b. to crumple
   c. to fasten a seatbelt

4. As for the sentence 'is some awful "unnatural" coupling in prospect?' (l. 66), the author implies
   a. Hamlet's desire to die together with his mother.
   b. Hamlet's desire to have a sexual relationship with his mother.
   c. Claudius' desire to kill Hamlet and his mother.

5. Which of the following could we have more 'lemon juice' from?

   a. 18th-century English literature

   b. modern English history

   c. John Donne's poems

ACTIVE LEARNING for Discussion

1. 第 1 パラグラフの *Uncle Tom's Cabin* や *On the Road* の例のように、読まれる時代や、個人の読む時期によって解釈が変わる例を、知っている文学作品や映像作品に当てはめて、ペアまたはグループで話し合ってみましょう。

2. 第 8 パラグラフのハムレットのセリフで、ハムレットがネロを引用したことについて筆者は二つの解釈をしています。それぞれどのようなものか明らかにし、特に後者についてどこまで同意できるか、ペアまたはグループで話し合ってみましょう。

3. 多様な解釈をできる限り引き出すような曖昧さが特徴的なテクストの例と、歴史や政治的なコンテクストがより重視されるテクストの例をそれぞれ考えて、どんなものがあるのかペアまたはグループで話し合ってみましょう。

 読むならまずこの一冊

ウィリアム・シェイクスピア『ハムレット』（白水社 U ブックス、岩波文庫、角川文庫、新潮文庫、ちくま文庫など他多数）
実際に作品を読んでみて、自分の読解が、列挙されたハムレット像のどれに一番近いのか、あるいはどれも当てはまらず新しい解釈となるのか確かめてみよう。また、本文で引用されている 'son/sun' の語呂合わせやハムレットのネロを引用したセリフの部分を、日本語訳ではどのように工夫しているのか（あるいは何を優先させて、何を犠牲にしているのか）考えてみるのも面白いだろう。

CHAPTER 3

ナラティヴとストーリー
Narrative/Story

イギリスの小説家 E・M・フォースター（E. M. Forster）は、ケンブリッジ大学での 1927 年の講演録『小説の諸相』の中で、「ストーリー (story)」というものの重要性を強調した。小説家とは何よりも「ストーリーを語る存在」なのだとフォースターは言う。それから 80 年後、同じくケンブリッジ大学で講演をした批評家フランク・カーモード（Frank Kermode）は、フォースターに言及しながら同様のトピックについて考察した。しかしカーモードは、ストーリーではなく「ナラティヴ (narrative)」という用語を用いたのである。ナラティヴとストーリーの違いとは何なのだろうか？　そして、どうしてナラティヴという用語がここ数十年の間にストーリーという言葉に取って代わることになったのだろうか？

 ## Pre-reading Vocabulary Check

日本語の意味に合う英文になるよう、次の中から適切なものを選びなさい。必要に応じて形を変えなさい。

> synonym · subject matters · doctrines · sophistication · objection ·
> ownership · implications · sequels

1. 『若草物語』には続編がふたつある。
Little Women has two _____.

2. 「国際テーマ」はヘンリー・ジェイムズの作品の重要な主題のひとつである。
The 'international theme' is one of the important _____ in Henry James' works.

3. 車を売りたいのなら、買い手に所有権を譲渡する方法を知っておく必要がある。
If you want to sell your car, you need to know how to transfer _____ to the buyer.

4. 洗練されていないことは必ずしも欠点とはかぎらない。
Lack of _____ is not necessarily a drawback.

5. 「昭和」はますます「昔」の類語になってきている。
'Showa' has increasingly become a _____ for the 'old days'.

6. 私はそのことに異議はありません。
I have no _____ to it.

7. 彼の発言にはしばしば性差別的な含意がある。
His remarks often have sexist _____ .

8. 従来と同じ学説を繰り返す以上のことをしなければならない。
You should do more than just repeat the same conventional _____.

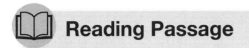

Reading Passage

1 Story and narrative: what's the difference? Story and narrative are not synonyms. Very simply, 'story' directs our attention to *what* is told. 'Narrative' directs our attention to *how* it is told – to technique, not subject matter.

2 Novelists themselves have always been fascinated by the technical 5 question of how they should go about their work. There was spirited debate in the eighteenth century as to whether the epistolary method (using letters) of novelists like Richardson, which 'wrote to the moment*', was more effective than Fielding's 'comic epic*' technique.

3 In *Bleak House*, Dickens bisected* the line of his story between an 10 omniscient narrator (an 'implied' Dickens*) and a personage* in the novel, Esther, writing autobiographically (anything but omniscient, Miss Summerson does not even recognise her own mother). Dickens, one senses, was trying the techniques out, as a person might go into a shoeshop and try on various footwear before buying two different pairs because he couldn't 15 make his mind up.

4 Historically the novel form became fully self-conscious on this matter with the publication of Henry James' 'Art of the Novel' prefaces to the 1907-09 New York edition of his work. The burden* of James' doctrine was simple: 'how' was God.   20

5 Narrative – the stress on *technique* The Jamesian doctrine can be demonstrated by reference to his best-known work, *The Turn of the Screw*, in which he offers an object lesson* on how it should be done. It was designed as a Christmas Eve 'gruesome' ghost story. There is a frame within the frame. Douglas, one of the narrators*, is telling his gruesome tale to a gathering of 25 guests. We listen with them. He opens a document

> 'in old, faded ink, and in the most beautiful hand.' He hung fire again. 'A
> woman's. She has been dead these twenty years. She sent me the pages in
> question before she died … She was my sister's governess,' he quietly said.
> 'She was the most agreeable woman I've ever known in her position; she 30
> would have been worthy of any whatever. It was long ago, and this episode
> was long before.'

The narrator goes on to read out the governess's narrative. It chronicles her superintendence* of two strange children in a sinister country house. Is the house haunted? Are the children possessed? Is the governess the paranoid 35 victim* of her own Gothic fantasies*?

6 The story builds to a violent climax – but gradually. It is the inexorable, wholly enigmatic process that grips and terrifies. James' point is that to get your effect (in this case blood-curdling* horror), you must twist the story in gradually, like a screw, not hammer it in like a nail.

7 The art of literature, Henry James tells us, lies in the telling, the *narrating*, not in what is told – the raw materials of fiction are, in themselves, just that: raw. Concentration on narrative has created a critical climate*; an orthodoxy* and a whole new set of players in the great game of fiction – implied readers, implied authors, unreliable narrators* (do we trust everything that Nelly Dean tells Lockwood in *Wuthering Heights*? Do we trust everything Lockwood tells us?).

8 None the less, with all this welcome sophistication, there remains a strong case to be made for 'story'. It is possible to 'over-narrate'. Try to nail something down* in a novel, said D. H. Lawrence, and you either kill the novel, or the novel gets up and walks away with the nail.

9 **The death of story-telling?**   There is another objection. A stress on 'narrative' over 'story' creates ownership – 'liens*', as lawyers call them. James, having put so much Jamesian 'art' into the work, 'owns' *The Turn of the Screw*. No one, by contrast, owns a fairy story like *Cinderella*. The Brothers Grimm or Walt Disney can pick it up and handle it very differently. No one owned the Oedipus legends. Sophocles owned *Oedipus Rex*.

10 The Marxist critic* Walter Benjamin (always more playful than most of his co-ideologues*) leapt on the 'capitalistic' implications of this distinction between public and private literary ownership. The novel (i.e. the story produced under modern capitalism), Benjamin asserted, represented 'the death of story-telling'. This startling paradox can be illustrated by the homely example of the 'dirty' joke. If, in a school playground, a boy (forgive the sexism) tells a chum* a 'good joke' – which he would never dare put on paper – and that chum tells another chum and so on, each – in the telling – will change the story in subtle ways.

11 By the usual Chinese Whispers* effect, it may well trickle back, in a week or so, to the original schoolyard teller ('Heard it, ages ago,' he ejaculates*, contemptuously*). But it may well be almost unrecognisable, what with the details it's acquired and lost, in its passage from mouth to ear. Who *owns* that story? Everyone and no one. The narration/narrator arrangement is unfixed. Each teller told it his way.

12 We can see this played out in newspapers. If there is a big story (the death of Diana*), every paper will lead with it – but each will report it differently. Is it the same story in *The Times, The New York Times,* or the *News of the* ₇₅ *World**?

⑬ Novelists, typically, take a robust* view on the matter. J. D. Salinger's last public act, for example, was to initiate a court to suppress an unauthorized* sequel to *The Catcher in the Rye*, called *60 Years Later: Coming Through the Rye*. What made it *his*? The narrating, stupid. ₈₀

② wrote to the moment：「（現在進行中の事柄に対して）臨場感をもって語る」18 世紀英国の作家サミュエル・リチャードソンが、知人に宛てた手紙の中で述べた言葉。

comic epic：「喜劇的叙事詩」18 世紀英国の作家ヘンリー・フィールディングが、『ジョゼフ・アンドリューズ』（1742 年）の序文で、自らの目指す小説のあり方を示した言葉。▶ Chapter 4 Epic

③ bisect：「二つに分ける」

'implied' Dickens：現実の作者ディケンズではなく、あくまで作品から再構成される「内包された作者（implied author）」としてのディケンズ。▶解説 implied author

personage：「登場人物」

④ burden：「要点」

⑤ object lesson：「実例」

Douglas, one of the narrators：ダグラスはあくまで手記を読み上げる人物であり、小説『ねじの回転』自体の語り手は、ダグラスの話を聞いている客人の中の一人である。

superintendence：「監督」

paranoid victim：「偏執症の犠牲者」

Gothic fantasy：「ゴシック的夢想」▶ Chapter 5 Gothic

⑥ blood-curdling：「血も凍るほど恐ろしい」

⑦ critical climate：「批評の潮流」

orthodoxy：「正統的な教義、通説」

implied readers, implied authors, unreliable narrators：「内包された読者、内包された作者、信頼できない語り手」いずれも物語論（ナラトロジー [narratology] ▶解説）の用語。▶解説 implied reader/unreliable narrator

⑧ nail something down：「固定する」この文脈では、'over-narrate' することによって過度に物語の意味を固定してしまうこと。

⑨ liens：「先取特権」

⑩ Marxist critic：「マルクス主義批評家」▶ Chapter 7 Base / Superstructure

co-ideologue：ideologue は「特定の主義を信奉する人たち」。co- は「共同」の意味をもつ接頭辞で、ここではベンヤミンが属していたとされるフランクフルト学派と呼ばれるドイツの社会思想家たちのことを指す。

chum：「（男同士の）親友」

⑪ Chinese Whispers：「伝言ゲーム」

ejaculate：「不意に叫ぶ」

contemptuously：「軽蔑を示して」

⑫ Diana：「元英国皇太子妃のウェールズ公妃ダイアナ（1961–97）」1997 年、パリでの交通事故で不慮の死を遂げ、大きなニュースとなった。

The Times, The New York Times, or the News of the World：*The Times* はイギリス、*The New York Times* はアメリカのそれぞれ大手新聞。*News of the World* はイギリスのタブロイド紙（煽情的な新聞）。

⑬ robust：「断固とした」

unauthorized：「非公認の」

Post-reading Vocabulary Check

➤ 日本語の意味に合う英文になるよう、次の中から適切な 動詞 を選び、必要に応じて形を変えなさい。

design ・ chronicle ・ haunt ・ initiate ・ grip ・ terrify ・ handle ・ suppress

1. 彼は仕事を失うことへの恐怖に取りつかれていた。

He was _____ by the fear of losing his job.

2. この科目は 1945 年以降のアメリカ文学への導入のためのものである。

This course is _____ to be an introduction to American literature since 1945.

3. 私は犬が怖い。

Dogs _____ me.

4. 我々は新たな行動計画に着手する必要がある。

We need to _____ a new plan of action.

5. この件は私に担当させてください。

Let me _____ this.

6. 彼は感情を抑えることができなかった。

He couldn't _____ his emotions.

7. その映画はある伝説的なブルース歌手の生活と仕事を記録している。

The film _____ the life and career of a legendary blues singer.

8. 彼女の声は私の心をつかんだ。

Her voice _____ my heart.

➤ 下記の 形容詞または副詞 =英英・英日の語義が成立するように、空欄を埋めなさい。

1. spirited = l □□□□□ , active, energetic 「活発な」

2. omn □□□□□□□ = all-knowing, all-seeing, almighty 「全知の」

3. au □□□□□□□□□□ ally = as an account of a person's life written by that person 「自伝的に」

4. gruesome = horrific, dre □□□□□ 「ぞっとする、身の毛のよだつ」

5. ag □□□□□□□ = pleasant, delightful 「感じのよい」

6. worthy = ad □□□□ ble, respectable, virtuous 「尊敬すべき、立派な、善良な」

7. sinister = seeming evil or dangerous, thr □□□□□□□□ 「不吉な、悪意のある」

8. in □□□□□□□ = relentless, impossible to stop or prevent 「容赦のない、不可避の」

9. en □□□□□□□ = mysterious, difficult to understand 「不可解な、得体のしれない」

10. st □□□□□□ = surprising, shocking 「びっくりさせる」

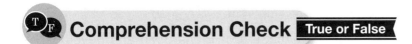

Comprehension Check `True or False`

下の英文が本文の内容として正しい場合は T、間違っている場合は F を選びましょう。

1. 'Story' is the term used to focus more on technical questions in the novel. (T / F)
2. *The Turn of the Screw* illustrates how Henry James puts emphasis on narrative.

   (T / F)
3. D. H. Lawrence argues for the importance of story and warns against concentrating on narrative too much. (T / F)
4. A fairy tale like *Cinderella* is open for everyone to remake, for no one owns the story. (T / F)
5. J. D. Salinger initiated a court battle because he did not think the sequel was well-written. (T / F)

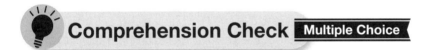

Comprehension Check `Multiple Choice`

本文の内容に照らして最も正しいものを a 〜 c の中から選んで○をつけなさい。

1. Which of the following is true about *Bleak House*?
    a. Dickens seems to have little interest in technical questions.
    b. There are two different types of narrators coexisting in the novel.
    c. Esther Summerson plays the role of omniscient narrator.
2. Which of the following is true about *The Turn of the Screw*?
    a. It is a story of a country house haunted by the ghosts of paranoid victims.
    b. The governess narrates her story in front of guests.
    c. James makes gradual twists in the story to get more effects.
3. Which of the following does NOT involve any ownership?
    a. *The Turn of the Screw*
    b. The Disney film *Cinderella*
    c. The Oedipus legends
4. The example of a big story in newspapers is similar to that of a joke in a schoolyard in the sense that
    a. the question of ownership is unfixed in both cases.
    b. both stories are based on sexism.
    c. the original story remains the same in spite of the Chinese Whispers effect.

5. Which of the following is NOT true according to the passage?

   a. Fielding supported the epistolary method of Richardson and developed it further.

   b. *Wuthering Heights* is an example of the novels which have unreliable narrators in them.

   c. Some objections have been made to the stress on 'narrative' over 'story'.

 ACTIVE LEARNING for Discussion

1. 第5パラグラフでは、*The Turn of the Screw* には 'a frame within the frame' があると指摘されていますが、それは具体的にどんなものでしょうか。筆者の説明や作品からの引用部分を分析して、物語の枠組みがどのようなもので、それがどのような効果を生み出しているか、ペアまたはグループで話し合ってみましょう。

2. 第9パラグラフに 'No one, by contrast, owns a fairy story like *Cinderella*. The Brothers Grimm or Walt Disney can pick it up and handle it very differently.' とあるように、『シンデレラ』の物語には時代や国を超えて様々なバージョンが存在しています。どのようなバージョンがあるのか、そしてそれらのストーリーはどんな点が異なっているのか、ペアまたはグループで調べて話し合ってみましょう。

3. 第10パラグラフでは、'the "capitalistic" implications of this distinction between public and private literary ownership' について言及されています。どうしてこの区別をすることが「資本主義的」と呼ばれるのか、ペアまたはグループで話し合ってみましょう。

 読むならまずこの一冊

ヘンリー・ジェイムズ『ねじの回転』（岩波文庫、光文社古典新訳文庫、新潮文庫など）
幽霊は本当に出現したのか？　それとも女性家庭教師の追い詰められた心が生み出した妄想なのか？「何が語られているのか」だけではなく「いかに語られているか」という 'narrative' の側面にも着目して読んでみよう。

CHAPTER 4

叙事詩
Epic

(*Gilgamish*) や『エヌマ・エリッシュ』(*Enuma Elish*)、『イーリアス』(*the Iliad*) は「今日のとんでもない出来事」のようなものでもなければ、単なるマッコール氏の不幸にも長引いた車旅のようなものでもなかった。逆説的なのは、うんざりするほど使われていながらもはや書かれていない（そして何世紀も書かれてこなかった）この用語が我々の口にたびたびのぼるのにもかかわらず、文学的な叙事詩はなくなってしまった、ということだ。

叙事詩とは現代の言説のそこかしこで、言うなれば意味を強めるのにやたら使われる言葉である。例えば、2009 年のロンドンの『デイリーメール』紙の見出し「デヴィーナ・マッコールが雪のなかで立ち往生した車から、家までの旅路がとんでもなく 10 時間もかかっている間中、ツイート！」など。ある研究によれば、2009 年はその新聞一紙だけでこの言葉は 850 回も使われていたことがわかった。『ギルガメシュ』

 ## Pre-reading Vocabulary Check

日本語の意味に合う英文になるよう、次の中から適切なものを選びなさい。必要に応じて形を変えなさい。

> lament・ingredients・friction・confidence・atmosphere・zenith・
> impediment・offspring

1. 彼を首相に任命したことによって、二国間では政治的あつれきが生じた。
His appointment as Prime Minister caused political _____ between the two countries.

2. 彼女の短気さが成功を妨げる障害になっている。
Her bad temper is an _____ to her success.

3. 恋愛結婚は現代の所産である。
Love-marriage is the _____ of modern times.

4. 彼女は自信に満ちている。
She is full of _____.

5. 彼の死から何年もたった後も彼女の悲しみは消えなかった。
Her _____ was great for many years after his death.

6. ナポレオンは全盛をきわめた。
Napoleon was at his _____.

7. 二国間には協調的なムードが感じられた。
A cooperative _____ prevailed between the two countries.

8. 『ハムレット』は優れた戯曲の条件をすべて満たしている。
Hamlet has all the _____ of a good play.

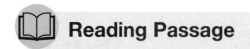

1 Literary epic: definitions Traditionally literary epic has four elements: it is long, heroic, nationalistic and – in its purest form – poetic. Panegyric* (extended praise) and lament are main structural ingredients. The first half of *Beowulf* (Britain's earliest surviving epic) is an extended
5 celebration of the hero's prowess* in defeating the Grendels, mother and child. The second half laments his death, having incurred fatal wounds in defeating the dragon that terrorizes his kingdom. In epic (see, for example, El Cid and Alfonso VI) there is, typically, friction between hero and monarch – prowess and inherited authority.

10 **2** Epic exudes* confidence about why human beings are on earth. It is, says the critic W. P. Ker, 'at ease in regard to its subject matter'. It knows what it is about and is firm in its moral judgements, particularly where villains are concerned. Leave it to modern writers, like John Gardner, in his 1971 novel, to sympathize with Mrs Grendel.

15 **3** It's easy to see why the epic should have wilted* in the uncongenial* atmosphere of recent times. The modern age does not like epically *long* works – particularly long works of poetry. As Edgar Allan Poe pointed out, the short lyric is the favoured form – works that can be 'read at a sitting*'. Thomas Hardy attempted, rashly, at the zenith of his fame, to write an 'epic drama',
20 *The Dynasts*. It was intended to be an 'Iliad of Europe from 1789 to 1815', with a heroic Napoleon at its centre. It is one of the grand failures of twentieth-century literature. For every thousand readers who read Hardy's short lyric poems, there is not one who wades through* *The Dynasts*.

4 Another impediment to modern epic is that modern life lacks 'heroes' – at
25 least, in the epic definition of the term. According to Maurice Bowra, epic (he was thinking primarily of Homer) commemorates 'those men who live for action and for the honour which comes from it'. Popular fiction (Tom Clancy, Andy McNab) is rich with such figures. But other than in the prostituted* *Daily Mail* sense of the term, there are no literary epics about them.

30 **5 Modern epic: a contradiction in terms?** Heroic heroes, and 'honour', make today's reading public uneasy. They are happier with anti-heroes, or downright unheroic heroes. Is Emily Brontë's Heathcliff a hero? Is Kingsley Amis' Jim Dixon a hero? Is Dan Brown's Robert Langdon a hero? Yes, in

terms of narrative centrality: no, in terms of the old-fashioned 'honour' we accord them. 35

6 Typically epic belongs to a great age that has passed and at which later ages look back nostalgically – with the sad sense that such greatness is gone for ever. The most venerable* epic that has survived to us, *Gilgamish*, can be traced back to 2,000 BC. It originated in what is now called Iraq: the cradle of Western civilization*. 40

7 British literature is founded on an epic, *Beowulf*, probably composed in the sixth century and transcribed (by an unknown monk) in the tenth. There were attempts to keep the genre alive with Milton's Christian epic, *Paradise Lost*, and mock-epics* such as Pope's *The Dunciad* (and his immensely popular translations of Homer and Virgil) in the early modern period. Since 45 then, nothing worthy of the name.

8 The United States is a young country, and its frontier struggles, as civilization spread westward, can be argued to have inspired the last vital manifestation of epic, in the form of the cinema of D. W. Griffith (*Birth of a Nation*) and the cowboy genre. Demonstrably the epithet 'epic' gravitates 50 towards screen heroes such as John Wayne. But not in his non-Western performances.

9 Another problem for the modern epic is the nationalistic origin of the genre – more particularly the select league of nations qualified to possess it. Epics are the offspring of 'noble and puissant nations', as Milton called them. 55 Could Luxembourg, or the Principality of Monaco*, however gifted its authors, host an epic? Could the nationally diffused* European Union have one?

10 When Saul Bellow asked his insolent* question, 'Where is the Zulu* Tolstoy, where is the Papuan* Proust?' he was, essentially, making the point 60 that only great civilizations have great literature. And only the greatest of great nations possess epics.

11 For a variety of reasons, epics are the dinosaurs of literature. They once dominated, by virtue of* sheer largeness, but now they are in the museum of literature, not the workshop. When, precisely, did they fade out – and the era 65 of 'books and newspapers' (as Bowra calls it) kick in* and make them forever impossible? Plausibly in the eighteenth century, with the rise of the novel – sometimes called the 'bourgeois* epic'. Can a novel transcend its bourgeois character and be truly epic? Or is the term, as it might seem, a contradiction

70 (like 'jumbo shrimp*'). A case can be made for* *Tom Jones, Middlemarch, War and Peace*, and above all – given its allusive title – James Joyce's *Ulysses*. The term fits slightly more easily than Davina McCall's car journey. But at the end of the day*, it is an allusion to the real thing, not the thing itself.

---

❶ panegyric：「称賛」
prowess：「武勇」
❷ exude：「(自信などを) あふれ出させる」
❸ wilt：「元気がなくなる」
uncongenial：「そぐわない」
at a sitting：「一気に」
wade through：「読み通す」
❹ prostituted：「安売りされた」
❻ venerable：「古い」
the cradle of Western civilization：「西洋文明発祥の地」
❼ mock-epic：「モック・エピック (擬似英雄詩)」 ▶解説
❾ Principality of Monaco：「モナコ公国」
nationally diffused：「国の寄せ集めである」 diffuse は元々「拡散する」イメージであるが、ここでは様々な国から成り立っていることを示す。
❿ insolent：「不遜な」
Zulu：「ズールー族の」 南アフリカ共和国最大の民族
Papuan：「パプア人の」
⓫ by virtue of：「…のおかげで」
kick in：「はじまる」
bourgeois：「中産階級的な」
jumbo shrimp：「大きな小エビ」 shrimp は prawn よりも元々小さなえびの意味なので、言語的に矛盾している。
A case can be made for ... ▶ **make a case for ...**：「…に賛成の論を唱える」
at the end of the day：「結局のところ」『ユリシーズ』で描かれる 1904 年 6 月 16 日の終わり (すなわち小説の終わり) も意識した表現になっている。

Post-reading Vocabulary Check

➤ 日本語の意味に合う英文になるよう、次の中から適切な 動詞 を選び、必要に応じて形を変えなさい。

---
defeat・inherit・commemorate・transcribe・gravitate・qualify・
dominate・transcend
---

1. 彼女はおばの財産を相続した。

She _____ her aunt's property.

2. 冬になるとたくさんの人がスキー場へ引き寄せられた。

In winter many people _____ to ski resorts.

3. その国はかつて白人が優勢を誇っていた。

The country used to be _____ by whites.

4. 3対0で相手を負かした。

We _____ our opponent 3-0.

5. その出来事は人間の経験を超えていた。

The event _____ human experience.

6. 彼女のスピーチは文字に書き写された。

His speech was _____.

7. これは最初の月面着陸を記念して後世に伝える彫像なのです。

This is a statue to _____ the first lunar landing.

8. 弁護士の資格を持っている。

I am _____ as a lawyer.

➤ 下記の 形容詞または副詞 ＝英英・英日の語義が成立するように、空欄を埋めなさい。

1. uncongenial = bad, dis □□□□□ able「好みに合わない」

2. r □□□ ly = recklessly, hastily「軽率にも」

3. venerable = a □□□□□□□「古い」

4. demonstrably = c □□□□ ly「はっきりと、明白に」

5. puissant = influential, p □□□□ ful「権力のある」

6. insolent = ar □□□□□□□「傲慢な」

7. a □□□□□□□ = referring, indicative「暗示を含んだ」

T F Comprehension Check True or False

下の英文が本文の内容として正しい場合は T、間違っている場合は F を選びましょう。

1. Modern people prefer short poems to epics.   (T / F)
2. Tom Clancy's novels can be called epic.   (T / F)
3. *Gilgamish* was written in 2,000 BC in what is now called Iraq.   (T / F)
4. Saul Bellow insisted that Papua New Guinea should have epics.   (T / F)
5. The sentence 'now they [epics] are in the museum of literature, not the workshop'
   (ll. 65-66) means that an epic is what we appreciate, not what we write. (T / F)

Comprehension Check Multiple Choice

本文の内容に照らして最も正しいものを a ～ c の中から選んで○をつけなさい。

1. Which of the following does NOT apply to the elements of an epic?
   a. short
   b. heroic
   c. nationalistic

2. Which of the following is true about *Beowulf*?
   a. It is sympathetic to Grendel and his mother.
   b. It is confident about why human beings are on earth.
   c. It is the oldest epic that has survived.

3. Which is true about modern epic?
   a. Jim Dixon lives for honour.
   b. Heathcliff is regarded as a heroic hero.
   c. Modern readers prefer anti-heroes to heroic heroes.

4. The epic the author appreciates least is
   a. *The Dynasts*.
   b. *Paradise Lost*.
   c. *The Dunciad*.

5. Which of the following is NOT a reason why the cinema of D. W. Griffith and the cowboy genre share the elements of an epic?

a. The United States is a young country.

b. The United States' frontier struggles influence them.

c. The United States has a great civilization.

 ACTIVE LEARNING for Discussion

1. 第 10 パラグラフの 'only great civilizations have great literature. And only the greatest of great nations possess epics.' という Saul Bellow の意見について、文学作品の執筆言語や市場・販路の問題なども考慮に入れながら、賛成か反対か、ペアまたはグループで話し合ってみましょう。

2. 日本の作品で叙事詩と呼ばれるものがあるか、あるとしたら本文で挙げられている特徴と同じ点や違う点を挙げて、ペアまたはグループで話し合ってみましょう。

3. 『指輪物語』や『ゲド戦記』、『ハリー・ポッター』などのファンタジー作品が叙事詩と呼べるか、共通する要素・しない要素を挙げながら、ペアまたはグループで話し合ってみましょう。

 読むならまずこの一冊

アーシュラ・K・ル＝グウィン『ゲド戦記』清水真砂子訳（岩波少年文庫）
世界の成り立ちから作り込み、ドラゴンや英雄的と言っていいキャラクターを登場させているこのファンタジー作品を読めば、叙事詩的なものを感じたり、あるいは現代にアップデートされた叙事詩だと感じるかもしれない。

CHAPTER 5

Gothic
ゴシック

暗黒時代とよばれる中世の先鞭をつけたゴート族（the Goth）による殺戮と破壊、その名を冠したゴシック文学（Gothic）は、全編を恐怖に満たしながらなぜ今日なお人々をかくも魅了するのだろうか……考えてみれば「ゴシック」とは全く奇妙な概念である。どんな街中の大きな本屋にも十中八九、「ホラー、ゴシック」と高々と謳う棚がある。人はすぐにスティーヴン・キング、ジェイムズ・ハーバート、アン・ライスあるいはディーン・クーンツを手に取れる（あるいはより高尚な向きならば、エドガー・アラン・ポー、エミリー・ブロンテ、メアリー・シェリーを）。もし「ゴート族の」代わりに、「ヴァンダル族の」「モンゴル遊牧民の」文学とあったらどうだろうか。ゴート族らは多くのことをなした（そのほとんどはひどい被害をもたらした）。彼らが例外的になさなかったのが文学である。さらに言うならば現在我々の手にラテン語文学がごくわずかしか残っていないのは、彼らの破壊嗜好が原因だ。パピルスと羊皮紙はかくも楽しげに燃やされたのである。

 Pre-reading Vocabulary Check

日本語の意味に合う英文になるよう、次の中から適切なものを選びなさい。必要に応じて形を変えなさい。

> sublimate · lust · associate · therapeutic · succession ·
> rational · seduce · coerce

1. その作家は自分の苦しみをその小説へと昇華した。
The writer ＿＿＿＿＿＿＿ her suffering into the novel.

2. 彼は自分の金銭欲を隠さなかった。
He did not hide his ＿＿＿ for money.

3. 日本では多くの人が桜の花を春と関連づける。
Many people in Japan ＿＿＿＿＿＿ cherry blossoms with spring.

4. 我々は立て続けに起こる汚職を大変恥ずかしいと思っている。
We are very ashamed of such a ＿＿＿＿＿＿ of corruption.

5. 姫はあの王子に言い寄られることを嫌っている。
The princess hates to be ＿＿＿＿＿ by that prince.

6. 社長はその条件で会社を売らされた。
The president was ＿＿＿＿＿ into selling his company due to the condition.

7. 多くの人が猫を飼うことは健康によいと考えている。
Many people find living with cats ＿＿＿＿＿＿.

8. 彼は理性的な判断を下すことを求められている。
He is asked to make a ＿＿＿＿ judgement.

Reading Passage

🔊 Audio 1-06

1 Why the Goths?   The Goths originated in Eastern Europe – well outside civilization. They warred for centuries against the Roman Empire and sacked* the Eternal City* in AD 410, ushering in half a millennium of the 'dark ages'. With the destruction of Rome there were no centralized institutions of law, no currency, no commerce beyond primitive barter*, no literature, no civilization. Dark indeed. As Richard Davenport-Hines says, 5

> 'The Goths became synonymous with warlike barbarism, 'carrying Destruction before them as they advanced, and leaving horrid deserts every where behind them', as Edmund Burke wrote in 1756*. Their love of plunder* and revenge ushered* in a dark age, and the word 'goth' is still associated with dark powers, the lust for domination and inveterate cruelty.' 10

How, then, did 'Gothic' become an everyday literary term?

2 According to Freud, the basic 'drives*' in the human psyche are destructive and violently appetitive*. We are born murderers and rapists. These primal 15 urges are, according to Freudian theory, sublimated into socially acceptable forms: the sadist's primeval knife becomes the surgeon's healing scalpel*. A price is paid. At some primeval level we'd rather cut throats than remove appendixes. In his essay 'Civilisation and its Discontents', Freud argues that the more civilized we become and the more distant from those primitive 20 drives, the unhappier we must necessarily be.

3 The attraction of Gothic literature is that it offers a therapeutic escape, safely imaginary, from the controls of order and reason. Hegel observed (thinking of history, not literature), that 'The Sleep of Reason Produces Monsters.' 25

4 But as row upon row on the bookstore shelf witness, much as we may respect reason, we also love monsters: at least in books we do. Monsters ravage* across the page in our favourite narratives, from Grendel's Mother, through Dracula, to Hannibal Lecter. (As played by Anthony Hopkins, Lecter was voted the most memorable monster in movie history by the American 30 Film Institute in 2003.)

5 Gothic and the Romantic Movement   Romanticism*, with its profound doubts about the Enlightenment*, found particular creative release in the 'sleep of reason'. The most popular monster to be created in the nineteenth century, Mary Shelley's Frankensteinian 'creature', is, from one angle, a protest against her philosopher father's* rationality.

6 Mary Shelley conceived* her story on the Swiss-French border, where Diderot had, 40 years earlier, launched his inflammatory *Encyclopaedia* into pre-revolutionary France. How, Shelley's fable* queries, did 'Reason' (as propagated by the French *philosophes**) degenerate into the 'Terror'? It is allegorized* in the rational scientist Victor's intended creation of his perfect man, not a second Adam*, as his maker hoped, but a monstrous freak:

> 'How can I describe my emotions at this catastrophe, or how delineate the wretch whom with such infinite pains and care I had endeavoured to form? His limbs were in proportion, and I had selected his features as beautiful. Beautiful! Great God! His yellow skin scarcely covered the work of muscles and arteries beneath; his hair was of a lustrous black, and flowing; his teeth of a pearly whiteness; but these luxuriances only formed a more horrid contrast with his watery eyes, that seemed almost of the same colour as the dun-white* sockets in which they were set, his shrivelled* complexion and straight black lips.'

7 A holiday from the constraints of reason? Gothic makes serious points in its sometimes extravagantly* unserious way (a best-seller of 2009, one recalls, was *Pride and Prejudice and Zombies* – it sold more that year than Austen's novel). Gothic aims to provoke radically irrational responses and then control them. It allows a little dark age in the mind. It also gives us moral space to consider the place of evil, violence and criminality in our scheme of things. And to indulge complex mixed feelings about them.

8 Is Hannibal the Cannibal attractive, or repulsive? Both. Take a poll* of the most glamorous and sexually attractive hero in British fiction and the bookmakers* would give you very short odds* on Heathcliff. He has been played by a whole succession of matinée idols*, from Laurence Olivier to Ralph Fiennes and Cliff Richard. He is to the classic Victorian novel* what James Bond is to the spy novel.

9 Consider, then, the episode in which – out of wholly malicious motives – Heathcliff seduces Isabella Linton and coerces her into marrying him. Nelly Dean, the housekeeper-narrator at Wuthering Heights, records Heathcliff saying that the first thing he did, on carrying his bride off*, 'was to hang up her little dog; and when she pleaded* for it, the first words I uttered were a wish that I had the hanging of every being belonging to her.'

10 You can do many bad things in English fiction and get away with it. But throttling your wife's harmless little dog is not one of them. It's in character. Later Heathcliff will beat up Isabella unmercifully – the last we see of her she has a black eye. She's lucky he doesn't do worse. He murders the owner of Wuthering Heights who stands in his way.

11 How can we align his psychopathic brutality and his Byronic* allure? The conventions of Gothic fiction – of which Emily Brontë is a leading practitioner – pull off* this trick. And in so doing they indicate how literature can reflect the perverse peculiarities of the human personality. You won't find it in Hegel.

1 sack：「略奪する」
the Eternal City：「永遠の都」ローマの異名。
barter：「物々交換」
...as Edmund Burke wrote in 1756：▶解説
plunder：「強奪」
usher：「先駆けとなる」
2 drive：「欲動」▶解説
appetitive：「欲求の」
scalpel：「外科用メス」
4 ravage：「破壊する」
5 Romanticism：「ロマン主義」▶解説
the Enlightenment：「啓蒙主義」▶解説
her philosopher father：ウィリアム・ゴドウィン（William Godwin, 1756–1836）のこと。
6 conceive：「思いつく」
fable：「寓話」
philosophe：「哲学者」特に、ディドロ、ルソー、ヴォルテールなど 18 世紀フランスの啓蒙思想家のこと。原義はフランス語で哲学者の意味。
allegorize：「アレゴリー化する」▶ Chapter 10 Allegory
a second Adam：「第二のアダム」フランケンシュタインはあくまで極められた自らの知性による「人間」の創造を意図していた。
dun-white：「灰褐色がかった白」
shrivelled：「縮んでしわが寄った」
7 extravagantly：「過度に」
8 take a poll：「票決を取る」
bookmaker：「賭けの胴元」
short odds：「ほぼ等しい賭け率」ヒースクリフが票を集める可能性が高いので、賭けとしての儲けは小さくなる。
matinée idols：「（特に 1930–40 年代の）二枚目俳優」
the classic Victorian novel：「古典的ヴィクトリア朝小説」▶解説
9 carry off：「運び去る、さらう」
plead：「嘆願する」
11 Byronic：「バイロン風の」▶解説
pull off：「うまくやってのける」

Post-reading Vocabulary Check

➤ 日本語の意味に合う英文になるよう、次の中から適切な 動詞 を選び、必要に応じて形を変えなさい。

> plead・remove・usher・witness・rave・reflect・align・aim

1. 犯人は許しを請うた。
The criminal _____ for forgiveness.

2. 我々は路上の大きな丸太をどかさなくてはならなかった。
We had to _____ a big log on the road.

3. そのデザインは新しいファッショントレンドの先駆けとなった。
The design _____ in the new trend of fashion.

4. その部隊は街を荒らして回った。
The troops _____ across the city.

5. この短編はその作家の才能をよく示している、
This short story _____ well for the writer's talent.

6. グラスはテーブルの縁に沿って並べられた。
The glasses were _____ along the edge of the table.

7. この色は画家の死への不安を映している。
This color _____ the painter's apprehension of death.

8. この論文の目的はフランス革命の真の意義を明らかにすることである。
This essay _____ to clarify the real significance of the French Revolution.

➤ 下記の 形容詞または副詞 =英英・英日の語義が成立するように、空欄を埋めなさい。

1. i □□□□□□□□□ = deep-rooted, incorrigible「常習的な、頑固な」

2. a □□□□□□□□ = longing「欲する」

3. primal = p □□□□□□□□ , f □□□□□□□□□□「原始の、根本的な」

4. n □□□□□□□□□ = automatically, inevitably「必然的に」

5. p □□□□□□□ = deep, great「深遠な」

6. g □□□□□□□ = appealing, seductive「魅力的な」

7. m □□□□□□□ = malevolent, evil「悪意の」

8. perverse = dis □□□□□□「ひねくれた」

🗪 Comprehension Check **True or False**

下の英文が本文の内容として正しい場合はT、間違っている場合はFを選びましょう。

1. The Goths left a brilliant literary legacy. (T / F)

2. Gothic literature is hardly popular these days. (T / F)

3. Sigmund Freud's theory would well explain why people are attracted to cruel and violent depictions in literature. (T / F)

4. The place where Mary Shelley got the idea of *Frankenstein* is totally irrelevant to the history of Western thought. (T / F)

5. One of the significances of Gothic literature is that it describes what is completely unconnected with human nature. (T / F)

Comprehension Check **Multiple Choice**

本文の内容に照らして最も正しいものを a 〜 c の中から選んで○をつけなさい。

1. Which of the following is true about the Goths?
   a. Literature is the only thing they dealt with respectfully.
   b. They produced a wonderful alternative after they destroyed Roman civilization.
   c. The atrocity and destruction by the Goths can be regarded as the very beginning of the "dark ages."

2. According to Freud, which of the following is NOT true about the human psyche?
   a. Human beings are essentially pacifistic even at the deepest level of the psyche.
   b. Today we are living in a world transforming our primal, sometimes violent, urges into much more socially acceptable ones.
   c. Psychoanalytically speaking, human beings can be feeling discontent with this highly civilized society.

3. The Gothic and the Romantic Movement are similar NOT in that
   a. they both were antipathetic to the absolutizing of reason.
   b. they both encouraged people to actually commit crimes.
   c. they both believed in a creative power of irrationality.

4. Reading Gothic fiction, it is most unlikely that

    a. the more abominable the protagonists are, the more attractive they seem to the readers.

    b. people find clues to solve the past murder cases which actually happened.

    c. readers feel released from the stress of living a rational life.

5. Emily Brontë can be regarded as a Gothic writer because

    a. she asserted a radically feminist claim on women's rights in her works.

    b. she integrated contradictory attributes into one character.

    c. she actually produced many famous actors' debuts.

 ACTIVE LEARNING for Discussion

1. 第5パラグラフに 'creative release in the "sleep of reason"' とありますが、なぜ非理性的であることが創造力につながるのか、ペアまたはグループで話し合ってみましょう。

2. 本章では、理性を重んじる啓蒙主義に対するアンチテーゼとしてゴシックやロマン主義を位置付けていますが（第5・6パラグラフ）、理性と非理性的想像力／創造力それぞれの、人間にとっての長所短所をペアまたはグループで話し合ってみましょう。

3. ゴシック文学を扱う本章ですが、フランス革命についての大著のあるバーク（第1パラグラフ）やディドロがフランス革命以前に『百科全書』を出版したこと（第6パラグラフ）など、フランス革命について間接的に言及されている個所があります。その理由をペアまたはグループで考えてみましょう。

 読むならまずこの一冊

メアリ・シェリー『フランケンシュタイン』（創元推理文庫、光文社古典新訳文庫など）

モンスターとは恐ろしいものなのか。一番罪深いのは作中誰／何であるのか？ 「ゴシック」の枠にとどまらない名作！

CHAPTER 6

文化

Culture

「もし我々が文化というものを真剣に受け取るとすれば、人間はただ空腹を満たすだけでは不十分なのであり、良質で際立った料理を摂らなくてはならない。（中略）煎じ詰めれば、生を価値あるものにするのは文化だと言うことすらできるのかもしれない。」著書『文化の定義のための覚書』（*Notes Towards a Definition of Culture*）のなかで、Ｔ・Ｓ・エリオット（T. S. Eliot）は書いている。遡ること50年前にハーバードの同窓生である哲学者、ウィリアム・ジェイムズ（William James）が、「生を価値あるものにするのは何か？」と題した講演で問いかけたことに対する、意識的な回答だった。文化は宗教なき後の空白を埋めることができる、とエリオットは主張した。そして文学は、国の文化を形作るための核心的な要素だった。

✎ Pre-reading Vocabulary Check

日本語の意味に合う英文になるよう、次の中から適切なものを選びなさい。必要に応じて形を変えなさい。

> urge・prejudice・heritage・uproot・homogeneity・archetypal・
> boundaries・devote

1. 災害のために、多くの人々が家や土地を失った。
Many people were ＿＿＿＿＿＿＿ by the disaster.

2. その本は、著者の人種偏見をあらわにしていた。
The book exposed the author's racial ＿＿＿＿＿＿＿ .

3. マザー・テレサはその生涯を貧しく持たざる者たちを救うことに捧げた。
Mother Teresa ＿＿＿＿＿＿ her life to helping the poor and dispossessed.

4. 彼女は日本の民族的、文化的単一性という神話を信じていた。
She believed the myth of ethnic and cultural ＿＿＿＿＿＿＿＿＿ of Japan.

5. 彼は客たちに、もう少し滞在してくれるよう強く勧めた。
He ＿＿＿＿＿＿ his guests to stay longer.

6. ピカソはキュビズムの典型的な画家である。
Picasso is an ＿＿＿＿＿＿＿ artist of Cubism.

7. 妻は結婚生活においても個人的なスペースや境界線を保つことを要求した。
The wife demanded personal space and ＿＿＿＿＿＿＿＿ in their marital relationship.

8. これらの塚は、アメリカ先住民の豊かな文化遺産の好例である。
These mounds exemplify a rich Native American cultural ＿＿＿＿＿＿.

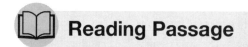

1 **Mass civilization, minority culture?** The idea of culture as *the* vital element in national identity was urged by Matthew Arnold, in his 1860s polemic, *Culture and Anarchy*. There had been, in the run-up to the Second Reform Bill of 1867*, working-class agitation. Some railings had been
5 destroyed in Hyde Park – not exactly the storming of the Bastille*, but a whiff of riot and revolution ('anarchy') was in the air.

2 Ideas about culture are invariably permeated by prejudice about class. Traditionally – and certainly for Matthew Arnold – culture is the property of society's 'civilized' class. This is not, necessarily, the toffs* (whom Arnold
10 cheerfully called 'Barbarians*', preferring as they did horses to Goethe*). Barbarians could, being moneyed, serve as useful patrons. So could wealthy members of the commercially enriched middle classes ('Philistines*'). The 'culture carriers' (*Kulturträger*), as Germans call them (Arnold was a fervent Germanist), will have benefited from class privilege, but float freely in an
15 ambience of 'sweetness and light*' *in*, but not necessarily *of* the upper and wealthier reaches of society. The lower middle classes and workers (the 'Populace*') were, in Arnold's view of things, irredeemably cultureless, as much a lost cause as the beasts of the field.

3 **Do only great civilizations possess culture?** Running through
20 Arnold's argument is an ineffable elitism. You cannot have what the Germans call *Hochkultur*￼ unless you have the trappings of humane education, civilized manners, good taste, and a broad cultivation that takes in travel, music, philosophy and an appreciation of cathedrals and oil paintings. Culture is a whole-mix thing. It is like an orchestra in which
25 literature is a soloist, but one that could not perform without an ensemble of different instruments around it.

4 James Baldwin, the African American novelist, described high culture eloquently, 100 years later, in his essay 'Stranger in the Village'. He contrasts his 'heritage' with that of the lowest Swiss peasant, ruefully noting
30 'The most illiterate among them is related, in a way I am not, to Dante, Shakespeare, Michelangelo, Aeschylus, Da Vinci, Rembrandt, and Racine; .... Out of their hymns and dances came Beethoven and Bach. Go back a few centuries and they are in full glory – but I am in Africa, watching the

conquerors arrive.' Note that Baldwin does not say that the 'illiterate' *create* the works of Dante, Shakespeare or Racine. But they are organically 'related' to them. What establishes that relationship? Rootedness. Culture, as in biology, is a living thing. Deracination* – uprooting – kills it, as surely as cutting kills flowers.

5 The twentieth-century advocate of elite art was the American immigrant turned Englishman T. S. Eliot. The basis of Eliot's idea of culture is 'homogeneity'. The necessary glue is supplied, primarily, by the Christian, royalist and Conservative traditions that Eliot had embraced on becoming English. Culture's bedrock was faith, and Eliot, notoriously, believed – as a corollary of this fideism*:

> 'The population should be homogeneous; where two or more cultures exist in the same place they are likely either to be fiercely self-conscious or both to become adulterate. What is still more important is unity of religious background; and reasons of race and religion combine to make any large number of free-thinking Jews undesirable.'

That last comment of Eliot's (uttered after World War Two) has given huge offence.

6 **'Working-class culture': a contradiction in terms?**   Even as he wrote, in 1948, voices were being raised against Eliotesque elitism. While accepting that literature/art was the product of class groupings, there were cogent defences of the intrinsic worth of working-class and 'popular' culture, and folk art. Spearheading the working-class cultural heroes was D. H. Lawrence – a miner's son who had never attended a proper university. Who was the archetypal Lawrentian hero? A gamekeeper* who wins an aristocrat's wife – Lady Chatterley – with such lover's lines as: 'Tha's got the nicest arse of anybody.'*

7 In the 1960s, works such as Lionel Trilling's *Beyond Culture* and Richard Hoggart's *The Uses of Literacy* fuelled a lively Anglo-American debate on the subject. Powerful voices from the left were demanding respect for culture that was neither elitist, provincial, metropolitan nor monocultural* and which had been too long suppressed or marginalized.

8 The debate formed into a school. 'Cultural Studies*' was grafted on to Humanities educational curricula and became a subject in its own right ('courses on Mickey Mouse and Danielle Steel' sneered the sceptical ranks of cultural traditionalists). While literature remained a principal interest, the focus was broadened – often to the point of total diffusion. Canon-busting* ('counter-culture*') became a competitive academic sport. The danger was that Cultural Studies, freed canonical boundaries, became a study of everything and anything. One professor, at Princeton, a star in the new academic firmament, devoted himself to the study of the TV weather channel.

9 Broadening of the cultural aperture* in this way, argued Allan Bloom, led, paradoxically, to what he called 'The Closing of the American Mind': 'What is advertised as a great opening is a great closing. No longer is there a hope that there are great wise men in other places and times who can reveal the truth about life — except for the few remaining young people who look for a quick fix from a guru.'

10 In the last decades of the twentieth century, with an arch-conservative in the White House, revolvers blazed as traditionalists fought back in the so-called 'Culture Wars*'. It was tweed jackets versus low-rider jeans at dawn*.

---

1 the Second Reform Bill of 1867：「イギリスの 1867 年の選挙法改正」イギリスとウェールズの一部の都市部に住む男性に選挙権が与えられた。
the storming of the Bastille：「(1789 年のフランスの) バスティーユ監獄襲撃」フランス革命の幕開けとなった。
2 toff：「めかしこんだ上流階級の紳士」
Barbarians：「野蛮人」▶解説
preferring as they did horses to Goethe：「ゲーテより馬のほうが好きな」
Philistines：「ペリシテ人」▶解説
sweetness and light：「甘美と光」▶解説
Populace：「大衆」▶解説
3 Hochkultur：「高尚な文化」
4 deracination：「根こそぎにすること、慣れた環境から隔絶すること」
5 fideism：「信仰至上主義」
6 gamekeeper：「森番」
'Tha's got the nicest arse of anybody'：「あんたいいケツしてんな」
7 monocultural：「単一文化主義的な、社会的・民族的文化の単一性を重視する」
8 Cultural Studies：「カルチュラル・スタディーズ、文化研究」▶解説
canon-busting：「キャノンを叩く、攻撃する」
counter-culture：「反体制文化」
9 aperture：「裂け目」
10 Cultural Wars：「文化戦争」▶解説
tweed jackets versus low-rider jeans at dawn：「新旧の価値観が衝突する一歩手前」ツイードのジャケットとローライズジーンズはそれぞれ伝統主義者と自由主義者を指す。

Post-reading Vocabulary Check

➤ 日本語の意味に合う英文になるよう、次の中から適切な 語 を選び、必要に応じて形を変えなさい。

---

agitation・permeate・bedrock・spearhead・adulterate・marginalize・
sceptical・guru

---

1. 投票は民主主義の基礎を形作る行為である。
   The act of voting forms the _____ of democracy.

2. 化学物質が浸み込んだために土壌が汚染された。
   The soil was polluted because the chemicals _____ it.

3. その役人は、政策が実際に施行されるかについては懐疑的だった。
   The government official was _____ about the enforcement of the policy.

4. マーティン・ルーサー・キング・ジュニアは先陣を切って公民権運動を指導した。
   Martin Luther King Jr. _____ the civil rights movement.

5. そのチョコレートは小麦粉やクズウコンなどの混ぜ物がしてあった。
   The chocolate was _____ with flour and arrowroot.

6. 彼女は若い女性たちにとってフィットネスの教祖のような存在だった。
   She was a fitness _____ to young women.

7. 彼の表情から動揺は読み取れなかった。
   His facial expression showed no sign of _____.

8. 排除された少数派のグループはたがいに連帯した。
   _____ minority groups formed solidarity with each other.

➤ 下記の 形容詞または副詞 ＝英英・英日の語義が成立するように、空欄を埋めなさい。

1. vital = e□□□□□□□□ 「不可欠の」

2. invariably = c□□□□□□□□□ , always 「変わらず、常に」

3. ineffable = i□□□□□□□□□□□ , unutterable 「言いようのない、言語に絶する」

4. e□□□□□□□□□ = articulately, fluently 「雄弁に、流暢に」

5. n□□□□□□□□□□ = unfavorably, infamously 「悪名高く、（悪い意味で）知れ渡るほどに」

6. i□□□□□□□□ = natural, inherent 「本源的な、内在的な」

7. lively = v□□□□□□□□□ , full of life 「活気に満ちた、潑剌とした」

8. c□□□□□□□□□□ = contentious, aggressive 「競争心に満ちた、好戦的な」

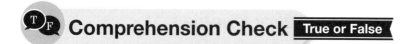

Comprehension Check **True or False**

下の英文が本文の内容として正しい場合は T、間違っている場合は F を選びましょう。

1. Matthew Arnold believed in the middle-class cultural values. (T / F)

2. According to James Baldwin, in Europe, even less sophisticated class groups are related to a distinct cultural tradition. (T / F)

3. Eliot's statement about monoculture caused considerable disagreement. (T / F)

4. Lady Chatterley is of working-class descent. (T / F)

5. You can study the TV weather channel as long as you don't belong to academia.

(T / F)

Comprehension Check **Multiple Choice**

本文の内容に照らして最も正しいものを a 〜 c の中から選んで○をつけなさい。

1. Which of the following is the least culturally sophisticated according to Matthew Arnold?

   a. Barbarians

   b. Philistines

   c. Populace

2. James Baldwin suggests that his cultural tradition was completely cut off because of

   a. a feudal system.

   b. a civil war.

   c. slavery.

3. What is the most important element in Eliot's insistence in cultural homogeneity?

   a. class

   b. religion

   c. language

4. Which of the following is NOT the accomplishment of the cultural debate in the 1960s?

   a. Marginalized cultural subjects found their voices in cultural criticism.

   b. Broader subjects of study were accepted within the scope of academism.

   c. Literary canon gained back its legitimacy.

5. Which of the following is closest to the author's opinion about Cultural Studies?

  a. Researchers should study everything and anything.

  b. By broadening subjects way too far, researchers have lost their academic focus.

  c. Academia should further pursue cultural relativism.

 ACTIVE LEARNING for Discussion

1. 導入文（p. 39）に引用されている、エリオットの「生を価値あるものにするのは文化だ」、という発言についてどう思いますか。ペアまたはグループで話し合ってみましょう。

2. 第 2 パラグラフ、第 3 パラグラフで出てくる 'Kulturträger' や 'Hochkultur' といったドイツ語の言葉は、どんな効果を意図して使われていると思いますか。ペアまたはグループで話し合ってみましょう。

3. この章では、ポピュラー・カルチャーやサブカルチャーなど、伝統的な文学批評では取り上げられてこなかった作品や事象を研究の対象とすることの是非や影響について議論されています。あなた自身はこの問題についてどう考えますか。ペアまたはグループで話し合ってみましょう。

 読むならまずこの一冊

上野俊哉／毛利嘉孝『カルチュラル・スタディーズ入門』（ちくま新書）
カルチュラル・スタディーズの歴史的成り立ちからどんなものを対象とするのか、日本での研究状況などをわかりやすく解説する入門書。

下部構造／上部構造

Base/ Superstructure

　下部構造／上部構造モデルはマルクス主義にその起源を持つが、ヨーロッパの社会主義の信条の一つとして、またリベラル派全般によって取り入れられている。1930年代の英国の炭鉱産業を専門的に扱った『ウィガン波止場への道』（*The Road to Wigan Pier*）において、ジョージ・オーウェル（George Orwell）は下部構造の考え方について、鋭く書いている。

　「お偉いさんが地位を保てているのは、炭鉱労働者たちが必死で働いているからに過ぎない。あなたや私やタイムズ文芸付録の編集者、なよなよした詩人やカンタベリー大司教や『幼児のためのマルクス主義』の著者、同志 X までひっくるめた全員が比較的まともな生活を送れているのは実のところ、地下に潜り、目元まで真っ黒にして、喉に炭塵をつまらせ、鋼のような腕と腹の筋肉で、シャベルを前へと動かしながらあくせく働く哀れな人々のおかげなのだ。」

 Pre-reading Vocabulary Check

日本語の意味に合う英文になるよう、次の中から適切なものを選びなさい。必要に応じて形を変えなさい。

> injunction・surplus・commerce・urbanization・manufacture・masses・
> deduction・inspection

1. シャーロック・ホームズは卓越した観察力と推理力を持つ。

Sherlock Holmes has prominent skills of observation and ＿＿＿＿＿＿＿＿ .

2. 彼女はそのキャリアを商工業の発展に捧げた。

She dedicated her career to the development of ＿＿＿＿＿＿＿＿ and industry.

3. 都市化がその地域の風景を一変させた。

＿＿＿＿＿＿＿＿＿ drastically changed the landscape of the area.

4. 日本では2年に一度車検が義務付けられている。

In Japan, we have a mandated car ＿＿＿＿＿＿＿＿ every two years.

5. その会社は宝飾品の製造に特化していた。

The company specialized in jewelry ＿＿＿＿＿＿＿＿ .

6. 裁判所はその本の出版差し止め命令を出した。

A court issued an ＿＿＿＿＿＿＿＿ blocking publication of the book.

7. その政治家は大衆に人気があった。

The politician was popular among the ＿＿＿＿＿＿ .

8. その店は衣服や靴などの軍の余剰品を売っていた。

The store sells military ＿＿＿＿＿＿ goods such as clothing and footwear.

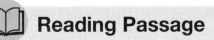

Reading Passage

1 Marxist* origins   Base/superstructure* is a temporal as well as spatial thing. Superstructural activity – writing literature, for example – is necessarily *secondary* in the historical – or even the day-to-day – sequence. Bertolt Brecht's earthy injunction, *'Erst fressen!'* ('Grub comes first!')* puts it bluntly. The echoing 'Culture second!' needs no saying. Marx himself put the 5 primary/secondary aspect more wordily in *A Contribution to the Critique of Political Economy*. It is a much-quoted passage:

> 'In the social production of their existence, men inevitably enter into definite relations, which are independent of their will, namely [the] relations of production appropriate to a given stage in the development of 10 their material forces of production. The totality of these relations of production constitutes the economic structure of society, the *real foundation*, on which arises a legal and political *superstructure*, and to which correspond definite forms of consciousness.'

2 Brecht is pithier* and Orwell more eloquent. But the key terms in Marx's 15 phraseology* are 'real foundation' and 'superstructure'. Literature is the product of what Marx elsewhere terms 'surplus value'* – disposable leisure time, money, and a full belly. The refined, Proustian belch* after the Brechtian grub. Moreover, as Marx observes, what is going on down below will affect what is happening on top. It is not a simple cause and effect. 20 Street violence can, for example, generate counter-revolutionary*, or escapist* literature. But, Marx insists, you cannot disconnect literature – or any other superstructural activity – from its host society.

3 Is it useful? Yes   There are attractive aspects to the base/superstructure idea. It neatly explains, for example, the hierarchy of cultural forms and 25 media in terms of economic and industrial progress and the wealth they generate. Dance, street theatre, oral poetry require little in the way of finance. They thrive, even in pre-history. A film like *Avatar*, which broke box office records in 2010, required $300m* in upfront finance and a technology (itself immensely expensive) that only became available in the twenty-first 30 century. The commercial theatre that made Shakespeare possible was itself made possible by the explosive economic energies, commerce, and industrial wealth among the middle classes released by London's urbanization in the

CHAPTER 7: Base / Superstructure   47

seventeenth century.

35 **4** The novel, the only major literary form whose birth we can confidently date, is congenital with early capitalism in the eighteenth century. The primal text, *Robinson Crusoe*, is plausibly an allegory of 'homo economicus*' – how an individual, with nothing but his inborn talent, makes himself a landowner and rich. Defoe's novel would not have been possible until circuits

40 of manufacture (printing) and supply (bookshops, libraries) and money to buy books (*Robinson Crusoe* cost the goodly sum of a guinea*) were available to a literate reading public. Why did we not have *Hamlet* or *Robinson Crusoe* (let alone *Avatar*) in the fifteenth century? Because the 'base' wasn't there to make them possible – any more than men could fly to the moon in 1869*.

45 **5 Is it too easy?**   The danger of base/superstructure is that it quickly becomes reductionist – it's too easy an explanation. Clear-cut division between the two vertical sectors (cake/icing on the cake) is nowadays generally regarded as 'vulgar' Marxism. New Marxists* have complicated the model (on which Marx himself devoted relatively little analysis) vastly and

50 unvulgarly.

6 A major source of complication is the relationship between producers of material value in the base ('hand-workers', as Victorians called them) and producers of immaterial 'consciousness' ('brain-workers') in the superstructure. Put bluntly, if you were Orwell's coal-miner, what would you

55 feel about the idle classes above ground with time to read *The Road to Wigan Pier?*'

7 The same problem was given a vivid illustration in H. G. Wells' 1895 novel, *The Time Machine*. In that story, the traveller uses his wonderful new machine to go to the year 802,701. There he discovers that humankind has

60 devolved into two contrary species: the effete* Eloi, who spend their lives in a kind of Garden of Eden, doing nothing but play; and the cannibalistic* Morlocks, slaving in a subterranean factory world, emerging only at night, to eat Eloi. The Eloi are, of course, versions of the *fin de siècle** decadents, notably Oscar Wilde and his followers. The Morlocks are what the

65 contemporary novelist George Gissing called 'Workers in the Dawn' – the labouring masses.

8 Is the relationship of base person and superstructure person necessarily antagonistic? Must those relegated by historical destiny to the base be either submissive worker bees or cannibals? What of those societies, and cultures that have no 'economic base'? Periclean Athens* could boast a Sophocles and an Aristotle, not simply because of their native genius, but because there were five slaves (and women, who, as Aristotle said, were the same thing) for every free man. Where is the slave's or woman's *Oedipus Rex*? ⁷⁰

9 The easy deduction that 'consciousness' is the exclusive preserve of the superstructure is, on closer inspection, untenable; similarly that 'production' is the exclusive property of the base. There is creativity at all levels of society. The superstructure also 'produces' – ideology and political thought, for example. That immaterial product affects, and transforms, what is happening throughout the whole body of society, top to bottom. In other words, superstructure can materially influence base, as well as vice versa*. ⁸⁰

10 It's stimulating. But at the end of the day the base/superstructure model is useful principally insofar as thinking about it leads us to discarding it as anything other than a metaphorical stepping stone to more interesting (super-superstructural?) things. Used this way, the idea serves a very useful purpose. ⁸⁵

---

❶ Marxist：「マルクス主義の」 ▶解説
Base/superstructure：「下部構造／上部構造」 ▶解説
'Erst fressen!' ('Grub comes first!')：「食うのが先だ！」 ▶解説
❷ pithy：「簡潔な」
phraseology：「語法、表現法、専門語」
surplus value：「剰余価値」 ▶解説
Proustian belch：「プルースト的なげっぷ」フランスの作家マルセル・プルースト (Marcel Proust, 1871–1922) が社交界に生きる上流階級の風俗を好んで描いたことから。ブレヒトの「食うのが先だ！」とは対照的な、基本的な欲求がすでに満たされた状態を比喩的に指す。▶ Chapter 4 Epic
counter-revolutionary：「反革命の、反動的な」
escapist：「逃避主義的な」
❸ $300m：「3 億ドル」
❹ homo economicus：「経済人、ホモ・エコノミクス」 ▶解説
guinea：「ギニー」現在の 1.05 ポンドに当たるイギリスの貨幣単位。
any more than men could fly to the moon in 1869：「1869 年に人類が月に行けなかったのと同じことだ」アポロ 11 号の月面着陸は 1969 年なので、その百年前の 1869 年という年と比べている。
❺ New Marxists：「新マルクス主義者」 ▶解説
❼ effete：「活力のない、無気力な」
cannibalistic：「食人主義の」
fin de siècle：「十九世紀末の」
❽ Periclean Athens：「ペリクレス時代のアテネ」古代アテネの黄金期と言われる。
❾ vice versa：「逆もまた同じ」

Post-reading Vocabulary Check

➤ 日本語の意味に合う英文になるよう、次の中から適切な 語 を選び、必要に応じて形を変えなさい。

---

constitute・affect・generate・thrive・complicated・transform・discard・serve

---

1. その絵本は青虫が蝶へと変化する様子を描いている。

The picture book depicts how a caterpillar _____ itself into a butterfly.

2. 私たちは電力を作り出すためのより持続可能な方法を見つけねばならない。

We need to find more sustainable ways to _____ electricity.

3. そのレストランは酒類を提供しない。

The restaurant does not _____ alcohol.

4. 飲酒は睡眠に悪影響を与えうる。

Drinking can negatively _____ sleep.

5. その委員会は 5 名のメンバーで構成されている。

Five members _____ the committee.

6. 彼女の恋愛関係は複雑だった。

Her relationship status was _____ .

7. 彼らはその可能性をあっという間に放棄した。

They _____ that possibility immediately.

8. 1920 年代には合衆国経済は繁栄した。

The US economy _____ in the 1920s.

➤ 下記の 形容詞または副詞 ＝英英・英日の語義が成立するように、空欄を埋めなさい。

1. b □□□□□□ = frankly「率直に言えば」

2. u □□□□□□ = prepaid, paid in advance「前払いの、前金で支払われた」

3. c □□□□□□□□□ = inborn, inherent「生得的な、もともと備わった」

4. p □□□□□□□□ = reasonably, credibly「妥当にも、納得のいく形で」

5. v □□□□□ = coarse, unrefined「粗野な、洗練に欠ける」

6. a □□□□□□□□□□□ = hostile, opposed「敵対する、対立する」

7. r □□□□□□□□ = downgraded, lowered「貶められた、価値を下げられた」

8. u □□□□□□□□ = undefendable, insupportable「(意見、考えが) 擁護できない、弁明できない」

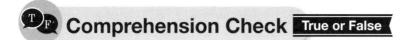

Comprehension Check — True or False

下の英文が本文の内容として正しい場合は T、間違っている場合は F を選びましょう。

1. Working at a coal mine is a superstructural activity. (T / F)

2. According to Marx, literary works are inseparable from the society they belong to.
(T / F)

3. A film like *Avatar* would not have emerged in the last century. (T / F)

4. Sometimes an argument revolving around base/superstructure gets too simplified.
(T / F)

5. *Oedipus Rex* was written by a slave. (T / F)

Comprehension Check — Multiple Choice

本文の内容に照らして最も正しいものを a 〜 c の中から選んで○をつけなさい。

1. Among the following authors, whose work best mentions the secondary status of literature?
- **a.** Bertolt Brecht
- **b.** Marcel Proust
- **c.** H. G. Wells

2. Which of the following is NOT at the heart of the wide reception of *Robinson Crusoe*?
- **a.** supply chain
- **b.** patrons providing money
- **c.** print culture

3. Which of the following describes the working class?
- **a.** brain-workers
- **b.** the Eloi
- **c.** the Morlocks

4. Sophocles and Aristotle could create their works partly because
- **a.** they understood the plight of the underclass.
- **b.** they did not have to do the 'base' work for themselves.
- **c.** they were not part of the rigid social system in Athens.

5. According to the author, which of the following is NOT true about base/ superstructure?

   a. Superstructural activities provide primary and essential work to society.

   b. Cultural forms reflect economic and industrial progress of their time.

   c. Not only base but also superstructure contributes to production.

 ## ACTIVE LEARNING for Discussion

1. 私たちが暮らす現代でいうと、下部構造／上部構造の具体例としてどんなものが挙げられますか。ペアまたはグループで話し合ってみましょう。

2. 本文に出てくるもの以外で、出版当時の経済・社会状況が色濃く反映されている芸術作品（文学、映像、絵画、音楽等）を思いつきますか。ペアまたはグループで話し合ってみましょう。

3. マルクスが言うように、文学や文化とそれが属する社会は切り離せないものだと思いますか。それとも、社会的、政治的価値から独立して存在する文学、文化はあり得ると思いますか。ペアまたはグループで話し合ってみましょう。

 ## 読むならまずこの一冊

テリー・イーグルトン『文学とは何か──現代批評理論への招待』大橋洋一訳（岩波文庫、上下巻）
文学批評理論の数々を概説しつつ、歴史や社会、イデオロギーが「文学とは何か」を決定する過程を鋭く論じる良質の入門書。

正典（キャノン）
The Canon

「キャノン（canon）」という語はキリスト教神学の用語として数世紀前に用いられるようになった。語源としては、「物差し」を意味する古代ギリシア語に遡ることができる。「聖書の正典」とは、正式に聖書のものと認められた文書を指す（正式なものと認定されず除外されたものは「外典」と呼ばれる）。時が経つにつれ、「キャノン」とは敬虔なカトリック教徒であれば誰もが読むべき原典のことを指すようになっていった。読むべきでないものは「禁書目録」に載せられた。このように、「キャノン」と「検閲」とはつねに密接に関係しており、権威によって決められるものである。この「正典（キャノン）」という概念は、どのように文学に適用されているのだろうか？　文学に適用して役に立つだろうか？

 ## Pre-reading Vocabulary Check

日本語の意味に合う英文になるよう、次の中から適切なものを選びなさい。必要に応じて形を変えなさい。

> anthology・emergence・fringe・eminent・immortality・manageable・
> prescribe・fluid

1. マシュー・アーノルドはヴィクトリア朝時代の著名な批評家である。
Matthew Arnold was an _____ critic in the Victorian era.

2. このメールに添付された所定の用紙に記入してください。
Please fill in the _____ form attached to this email.

3. 仕事量をもっと管理しやすくストレスの少ないものにする方法を見つける必要がありますね。
You need to find out a way to make your workload more _____ and less stressful.

4. 子供向けの詩の新しい選集を出版しようと思っています。
I am planning to publish a new _____ of poems for children.

5. 流動的な政治状況が人々を不安にさせている。
The _____ political situation makes people uneasy.

6. 彼は霊魂の不滅についての強い信念を持っている。
He has a strong belief in the _____ of the soul.

7. トーキー映画技術の出現がハリウッドの黄金期への道を開いた。
The _____ of sound film technology paved the way for the Golden Age of Hollywood.

8. 社会の周辺に生きる人々はたえず虐げられてきた。
People living on the _____ of society have been constantly oppressed.

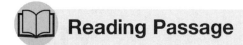

Reading Passage

1 **What is a literary canon?**   Around 30 years ago, the term 'canon' was imported to cover that nucleus of literature that was worthy of study at university, or of immortality in 'classic' reprint libraries (e.g. Penguin Classics*), or that would be prescribed on 'Great Books 101*' foundation courses, or found in the anthologies of literature marketed for educational institutions. Before the 1960s, the term would have meant nothing to well-read* people, as regards the literature they read, or were expected to read if they wanted the respect of their peers.

2 The literary canon has since become the most exclusive of clubs. Entrance is a fiercely contested matter, leading to 'canon wars*'. The canon's central membership (Shakespeare, Virginia Woolf, for example) is fixed for long periods, but not immutable. Even Shakespeare cannot be certain of always holding his place. At the fringes, it is as fluid and fuzzy as this week's best-seller lists. Are H. G. Wells, Theodore Dreiser or Rebecca West in there? Sometimes yes, sometimes no.

3 Educationally, the canon exists primarily to winnow out from the chaff* what Arnold calls 'the best that has been thought and said in the world': literature's richest harvest. There is, however, a secondary, hardly less important function. One 'consumes' literature, but unlike other consumables* (yesterday's hamburger, for example), it does not disappear once consumed, digested and excreted*. Literature accretes*.

4 In Chaucer's *The Canterbury Tales*, it is a matter of wonderment that the Clerk (the term meant something akin to our word 'scholar') had half a dozen books on his study bookshelf. That comprised most of what was available in the fifteenth century. With the Google Library Project's* arrival in the second decade of the twenty-first century, the modern clerk will have access to 15 million volumes in the palm of his hand.

5 There was no need for a 'literary canon' until the arrival of printing had enlarged the store of available literature from a hillock* to a mountain. The canon tends to be fixed in size; the apocrypha* – or non-canon – grows inexorably. *Vita brevis, ars longa*, says the classical* proverb: 'Life is short, art is long'. The problem is, it gets longer all the time.

6 **Early literary canon-making**   When Samuel Johnson, at the behest of* the London booksellers, compiled his *Lives of the Most Eminent Poets,* in the mid-eighteenth century, the epithet*, and the limited number (52 – one for every week of the year), represented a canonical procedure. It was, however, at the end of nineteenth century, with the emergence of a truly 'mass' literary culture, that canonisation* got going in force*. It took the form of classic reprint libraries (some, like Everyman* and World's Classics*, still survive) that effectively reduced what every 'well-read' citizen should read to a manageable hundred or so texts. For the student and pupil, anthologies such as Palgrave's 'Golden Treasuries' of verse* established themselves. At the same period in the 1890s, the best-seller list appeared. It too thinned out* the 'must-reads' of the moment into a manageable quantum*. Reduction was the driving force.

7 The canon and education   One of the attractions of the study of classics in schools and universities has always been the small size and fixity of the corpus*. Virtually the whole of classical Latin and Greek canonical literature can be contained on one CD disc. And, of course, it never grows. So too with Anglo-Saxon poetry*, which until a few decades ago was the foundation element in English studies.

8 Modern literature is a much less compactable* thing. There are currently around 150,000 titles published every year in the two major English-speaking markets. Some 10 per cent of those are classified as 'literature', swelling the two million or so literary titles already stored in the British Library* and the Library of Congress* (and, imminently*, on Google). A modern-day clerk would need to live to the age of Methuselah to read even a fraction of them.

9 Universities, schools and the authorities that set up such things as the 'National Curriculum*' have become adept at* thinning down* the canon to anorexic* proportions. A Great Books one-semester course will typically, in the US higher education system, allow some 90 to 100 hours' reading. At three minutes a page for prose, and ten minutes for verse, that gives you time – as the calculator glumly* estimates – to read *Moby-Dick* and *Hamlet*. So you prescribe a chapter here, a chapter there, a short poem or an anthology (like the best-selling Norton* range) that offers manageable excerpts.

10 It's nonsense, of course. A Victorian fiction* course, at the best universities in the Anglo-American world, will prescribe *Hard Times, Silas Marner, Tess*

70 *of the d'Urbervilles* and *Jane Eyre* and call it 'Victorian Fiction'. In fact these half-dozen or so texts give no more idea of what the 70,000 or so works in the field represent than six pebbles* will tell you what Chesil Beach* looks like. But what option does pedagogy* have?

11 The educational canon is one among many. There are 'alternative canons',
75 'queer* literature canons', 'feminist* canons', 'science fiction canons' – as many canons as there are specialist interest or affiliation groups*. There are national variations. *War and Peace* may be canonical for Russians; is it as canonical for – say – the French, who may, prejudicially, have a very different idea of Napoleon from Tolstoy?

1 Penguin Classics:「ペンギン・クラシックス」出版社のペンギン・ブックスが 1946 年に立ち上げた、古今東西の古典的名作を出版するシリーズ。
Great Books 101:「世界の名著入門」主に米国の大学で用いられている科目名のナンバリングシステムにおいて、'101'は当該分野の入門授業を指す。
well-read:「本をよく読む、博識の」
2 canon wars:「正典論争」▶解説
3 winnow out from the chaff:「(穀物を) もみ殻から選り分ける」
consumable:「消耗品」
excrete:「排泄する」
accrete:「蓄積される、増大する」
4 the Google Library Project:「グーグル図書館プロジェクト」グーグルが世界の主要な図書館の蔵書をデジタル化し、検索可能にするという計画。
5 hillock:「小山」
apocrypha:「外典」
classical:「古代ギリシア・ローマの」
6 at the behest of:「～の頼みで」
epithet:「形容句」この場合、*Lives of the Most Eminent Poets* の 'most eminent' という句を指す。
canonisation:「正典化」▶解説 canon-making/canonisation
get going in force:「本格的に始まる」
Everyman:英国で 1904 年に創刊された、古典の廉価版シリーズ。エヴリマン叢書 (Everyman's Library)。
World's Classics:英国で 1901 年に創刊された、古典の廉価版シリーズ。
Palgrave's 'Golden Treasuries' of verse:「パルグレイヴ英詩珠玉集」正式タイトルは *The Golden Treasury of English Songs and Lyrics*。英国の詩人フランシス・ターナー・パルグレイヴ (Francis Turner Palgrave, 1824–97) が 1861 年に初めて編纂した詩のアンソロジー。
thin out:「間引きする」
quantum:「量」
7 corpus:「(書かれた文献の) 集積」
Anglo-Saxon poetry:5 世紀半ば頃から 1066 年の「ノルマン征服」までにわたる約 600 年の期間 (アングロ・サクソン時代) の、古英語 (Old English) で書かれた詩。
8 compactable:「圧縮できる」
the British Library:「大英図書館」
the Library of Congress:「米国国会図書館」

imminently：「差し迫って」

⑨ National Curriculum：「国が定める教育カリキュラム」

adept at：「〜に熟達して」

thin down：「間引く、切り詰める」

anorexic：「食欲不振で痩せ細った」

glumly：「憂鬱そうに」

Norton：「ノートン社」米国の出版社。英語圏文学をはじめとする様々なジャンルのアンソロジーの出版で有名。

⑩ Victorian fiction：「ヴィクトリア朝小説」

pebble：「小石」

Chesil Beach：「チェジルビーチ」英国南部にある 18 キロメートルに及ぶ長大な砂利の海岸堤。

pedagogy：「教育法」

⑪ queer：「クィアの」現在では性的マイノリティ全般を指す総称として広く用いられている語。

feminist：「フェミニズムの」▶ Chapter 15 Sexual Politics

affiliation group：「共通の属性をもとにつくられる集団」

Post-reading Vocabulary Check

➤ 日本語の意味に合う英文になるよう、次の中から適切な 動詞 を選び、必要に応じて形を変えなさい。

| market · digest · comprise · enlarge · compile · reduce · swell · store |

1. そのアルバムは過去 10 年間のさまざまな未発表録音からまとめられた。

The album was _____ from various unreleased recordings from the past ten years.

2. ピューレは小さな子どもにも消化しやすい。

Purees are easy for small children to _____ .

3. 私はいつもコーヒー豆を冷蔵庫に保存している。

I always _____ coffee beans in the fridge.

4. 映画を英語字幕で観ることは語彙を増やすのに役立つ。

Watching films with English subtitles helps you _____ your vocabulary.

5. 会員数は約 250 人まで増大した。

Membership has _____ to about 250.

6. タバコをやめることは心臓疾患にかかるリスクを減少させる。

Giving up smoking _____ the risk of heart disease.

7. 合衆国のいくつかの州では、マリファナは合法的に嗜好用として生産され販売されている。

In some states in the US, marijuana is legally produced and _____ for recreational use.

8. この DVD ボックスセットはそのドラマのシーズン 2 の全エピソードを含んでいる。

This DVD box set _____ all the episodes from Season 2 of the drama.

➤ 下記の 名詞、形容詞または副詞 ＝英英・英日の語義が成立するように、空欄を埋めなさい。

1. p □□□ = fellow, equal, companion 「仲間、同僚」

2. immutable = fixed, unch □□□□ able 「不変の」

3. f □□□□ = vague, indistinct 「境界があいまいな」

4. akin = related, si □□□□□ , analogous 「類似して」

5. pro □□□□□□ = operation, process 「処置」

6. c □□□□□□ ly = presently, now 「現在のところ」

7. f □□□□ ion = fragment, piece, portion 「一部分、断片」

8. ex □□□□□ = extract, passage 「抜粋」

Comprehension Check **True or False**

下の英文が本文の内容として正しい場合は T、間違っている場合は F を選びましょう。

1. There has been much debate over the membership of the literary canon.　（ T / F ）

2. The author has no doubt that Shakespeare will hold his place as one of the canonical authors.　（ T / F ）

3. The Clerk in *The Canterbury Tales* has more books than modern scholars.　（ T / F ）

4. *War and Peace* is canonical for both the Russians and the French.　（ T / F ）

5. There are multiple canons according to the topic of interest.　（ T / F ）

 Comprehension Check **Multiple Choice**

本文の内容に照らして最も正しいものを a ～ c の中から選んで○をつけなさい。

1. Among the following authors, who is traditionally regarded as the most canonical?
   a. Virginia Woolf
   b. H. G. Wells
   c. Rebecca West

2. Which of the following was the first turning point in history that eventually led to various attempts of literary canon-making?
   a. the development of the higher education system
   b. the arrival of printing
   c. the emergence of mass literary culture

3. Which of the following is NOT part of the reason why reduction became the driving force of canon-making?
   a. the growth of the literary corpus over time
   b. the expansion of literary marketplace
   c. the decrease in the number of well-read people

4. According to the author, which of the following is the ideal way to make the amount of reading manageable in a college course?
   a. offering a series of excerpts of longer texts
   b. prescribing full texts of a few representative works
   c. neither of the above

5. Which of the following is NOT true according to the passage?

   a. The term 'canon' did not draw much attention in educational institutions until the 1960s.

   b. The canonical texts in English studies traditionally include Anglo-Saxon poetry.

   c. With the arrival of the Google Library Project, the idea of literary canon becomes no longer necessary.

 ACTIVE LEARNING for Discussion

1. 本文中で挙げられていたキャノンの存在意義と特徴をペアまたはグループで話し合い、改めて整理してみましょう。

2. 第4パラグラフでは、Google Library Project が今後の学問や社会にもたらすであろう影響について言及されています。Google Library Project とはどのようなプロジェクトなのかを調べ、その利点と問題点についてペアまたはグループで話し合ってみましょう。

3. 本文では英文学の例が紹介されていましたが、日本文学においてキャノンとされている作品にはどのようなものがあるでしょうか。また、日本文学のキャノンを定めるのに大きな影響をおよぼしているものは何でしょうか。ペアまたはグループで話し合ってみましょう。

 読むならまずこの一冊

平石貴樹編訳『アメリカ短編ベスト 10』（松柏社）
アメリカ文学の正典とされている作家たちの作品に短編を通じて触れることができる最良の実地体験型米文学入門書。くわえて、自らの選定した作品を「ベスト 10」と銘打つ編訳者のふるまいに、本文中で述べられているキャノン形成の意義の実例を見て取ることができる。

CHAPTER 9

ジャンル

Genre

混乱を避けるため、常に売れ筋であるフィクションに関しては、「名作」、「ゲイと官能」、「ロマンス」、「ＳＦとホラー」、「ティーン」、「犯罪小説」のセクションが大体設けられている。商業の観点では、事実上これがジャンルを表しており、受容がそれを創りあげる。かつては特定の男性客向けに「ウェスタン」セクションが設けられている店もあったが、そのジャンルはほぼ消滅してしまった。しかしグラフィック・ノベルなどの新しいジャンルが出てきてその空白を埋めている。

普段私たちが何気なく使っている「ジャンル」という言葉。しかしジャンルの境界はしばしば曖昧で、その存在意義も様々である。作家に、出版社や本屋に、そして私たち読者に、ジャンルはいったい何をもたらしてくれるのだろうか？

ジャンルという言葉の意味合いは、書籍業界における立ち位置によって変わってくる。小売店では陳列や配置に関わる。どんなに小さな本屋にも数千に及ぶ異なる商品が並んでいる。

Pre-reading Vocabulary Check

日本語の意味に合う英文になるよう、次の中から適切なものを選びなさい。必要に応じて形を変えなさい。

> pragmatic · fellow · would-be · dedicated · analogue · association ·
> practitioners · devotees

1. クロード・モネは印象主義を実践したもっとも有名な画家の一人である。
Claude Monet is one of the most famous _____ of Impressionism.

2. その歌手は多くのミュージシャン志望の若者たちに影響を与えてきた。
The singer has inspired many young _____ musicians.

3. この生産システムは現代における奴隷制の類似物と見なされうる。
This production system can be considered as a modern _____ of slavery.

4. 実際的な観点からすると、銃規制はアメリカでは難しい。
From a _____ standpoint, gun control is difficult in the US.

5. この協会は 2011 年に設立されました。
This _____ was established in 2011.

6. 仕事で成功できるかは、仕事仲間とうまくやっていく能力にかかっている。
Our success at work depends on our ability to get along with _____ workers.

7. その映画シリーズの愛好家たちでさえ最新作は気に入らなかった。
Even _____ of the film series did not like the latest installment.

8. 私の両親はマンチェスター・ユナイテッドの熱心なファンです。
My parents are _____ fans of Manchester United.

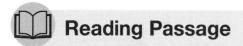

Reading Passage

Audio 2-01

1 Genre and book commerce   For the bookseller, genre is a pragmatic question of what to put where. It throws up occasional problems. Does, for example, Margaret Atwood's *The Handmaid's Tale* (which won a Hugo and a Nebula* – the two top SF prizes) go into the science fiction section, alongside
5 Asimov? Or the modern classics section, alongside Achebe?

2 For the genre author*, the term means something different. It's a kind of club, with a distinct set of rules, conventions, styles and fashions. In 1928, S. S. Van Dine drew up twenty rules for the crime writer, of which the first (and most inviolable) is: 'The reader must have equal opportunity with the
10 detective for solving the mystery. All clues must be plainly stated and described.'

3 Within the rules, there is a degree of freedom. But there is a core of shared tools and subject matter. You can pick up ideas, gimmicks, styles from fellow club members.

15 **4** If some innovative genre writer, like Robert Traver, comes up with the idea of the legal thriller* (*Anatomy of a Murder*, 1958), it will be picked up and recycled profitably (most profitably by John Grisham). A breakthrough MacGuffin (as Alfred Hitchcock called the plot gimmick that grips the film audience) may also be developed, creatively.

20 **5 Genre and the imitative author**   Me-tooism* is sanctioned, and even encouraged. Mills and Boon*, for example, have established sub-genres around the doctor-nurse scenario, the Georgette Heyer-style Regency romance*, or the 'governess tale'.

6 The major imprints* publish rule books, or templates, for would-be
25 authors. Readers want the cosily familiar rather than the strange.

7 Often writers of genre hang out together socially: as did the Detective Writers Club in the 1930s. They set up associations with prizes for outstandingly proficient fellow writers in their genre, such as the Edgar* (named after the 'inventor' of the detective story, Edgar Allan Poe) or the
30 Hugo (named after the 'inventor' of the term 'science fiction', Hugo Gernsback).

8 These genre prizes will typically be announced and awarded at large conventions, such as Worldcon (World Science Fiction Convention)*, with thousands of 'fans' in attendance. At Worldcon they like to dress, *Galaxy*
35 *Quest*-style, as their favourite SF characters.

9 It is a feature of genre that it mobilises large numbers of dedicated readers, who form affiliation sub-groups of their own* (nowadays by website, and web-based 'fanzines*'). Readers tend to be voracious consumers of their preferred fictional fare*. Surveys suggest that devotees of science fiction and crime read up to a dozen titles a month. Genre writers tend, in response, to be prolific. Barbara Cartland had a life score of some 600 titles, aided by a team of amanuenses*, turning out her pink and fluffy romances with the efficiency of a Japanese widget* factory.

10 Is genre a fiction-only thing? It's convenient to think of genres (science fiction, romance, PI* detective fiction, etc.) as empty boxes, waiting to be filled. But some precision is required. The novel is not, by most definitions, a 'genre' but a 'form'. It is a larger box that contains genres, Russian doll-style*.

11 Does 'poetry' contain genres? Does drama? Aristotle talks of comedy and tragedy as dramatic styles. Are epic*, lyric, satire, elegy *genres*? Arguably they are, but the term does not sit easily. Fiction is where the word seems most at home. There are, currently, five popular fictional genres in full production: romance (including historical romance), science fiction and fantasy, horror, thriller and crime.

12 Most practitioners stay within their box. Some, like Stephen King (who has written in all five genres – including a version of the Western, with his 'Gunslinger' saga) move around. But so brand-loyal are fans that genre writers prudently do not vary their stock in trade* too much. It is plausible to see 'pornography' as a genre – although it has migrated largely to visual and graphic forms.

13 There are, roughly speaking, two grand theories of how the imaginative energies of creative fiction disseminate themselves. One is a version of 'trickle-down'. A 'master' like Henry James rewrites the rules for fiction, and disciples* learn from him. An alternative view (favoured by the Russian formalists*) is that the energies explode from below, volcanically.

14 The second of these theories is the more plausible. Genre, that is, is the magma in which literature finds its primal existence. Analogues for Salman Rushdie's magic realism* in *Midnight's Children* (the inter-clairvoyance*, for example, of the children born at the moment of India's independence in 1947) are usefully looked for not in Henry James' *What Maisie Knew*, but in John Wyndham's *Village of the Damned* (published, originally, as *The Midwich*

Cuckoos).

75 **15** One of the more interesting literary frontiers is that where hard-boiled* genre melts into 'high' literature. A. S. Byatt's *Possession: A Romance*, for example, which blends critical theory, Victorian scholarship and traditional female romance. Another striking example is Paul Auster, whose *City of Glass* is offered as a 'metaphysical detective story'. Its narrative 'hook' is a

80 midnight phone call: 'It was a wrong number that started it, the telephone ringing three times in the dead of night, and the voice on the other end asking for someone he was not.'

16 The not-someone is 'Paul Auster, of the Paul Auster Detective Agency'. The recipient of the call is Daniel Quinn, who writes detective fiction (under

85 the pseudonym* William Wilson) but who, none the less, pretends, for reasons he himself cannot explain, to be Paul Auster and takes on the case. Genres bend. None the less, there was enough of the old-fashioned page-turner* for *City of Glass* to be nominated for an Edgar. Jacques Derrida has given this melting of boundaries a typically Derridean term:

90 degenerescence*.

---

1 a Hugo and a Nebula：「ヒューゴー賞とネビュラ賞」 ▶解説
2 genre author：「ジャンル作家」特定のジャンルに特化した作家。
4 legal thriller：「法廷もの」
5 me-tooism：「模倣主義」
Mills and Boon：「ミルズ＆ブーン」英国の出版社 ▶ Chapter 1 Mimesis
Regency romance：「リージェンシー・ロマンス」英国の摂政時代（1811-20）の頃を舞台としたロマンス。
6 major imprint：「大手の出版ブランド」
7 the Edgar：「エドガー賞」 ▶解説
8 Worldcon (World Science Fiction Convention)：「ワールドコン（世界ＳＦ大会）」 ▶解説
9 affiliation sub-groups of their own：ここでは「諸々の同人グループ」を指す。
fanzine：「ファンジン」ファンが作る同人誌。
fare：「料理、食べ物」
amanuenses（複）(amanuensis（単))：「執筆アシスタント」
widget：「小さい機械装置、部品」
10 PI：「私立探偵」private investigator の略
Russian doll-style：入れ子状を指す。マトリョーシカ人形の構造。
11 epic：「叙事詩」 ▶ Chapter 4 Epic
12 stock in trade：「いつものやり方」
13 disciple：「弟子、門弟」
Russian formalists：「ロシア・フォルマリスト」 ▶ 解説
14 magic realism：「マジックリアリズム」 ▶解説
inter-clairvoyance：「相互千里眼」
15 hard-boiled：「ハードボイルド」 ▶解説
16 pseudonym：「偽名」
page-turner：「どんどんページをめくらせるおもしろい本（の要素)」
degenerescence：「頽廃」 ▶解説

Post-reading Vocabulary Check

➤ 日本語の意味に合う英文になるよう、次の中から適切な 動詞 を選び、必要に応じて形を変えなさい。

mobilise・turn・migrate・favour・sanction・hang・take・disseminate

1. その工場は一日に数百万本の鉛筆を生産している。

The plant _____ out millions of pencils a day.

2. 彼女はその小説を日本語に翻訳するという難しい仕事を引き受けた。

She _____ on the difficult task of translating the novel into Japanese.

3. この宗教では飲酒は許されていない。

The consumption of alcohol is not _____ in this religion.

4. フェイクニュースはソーシャルメディアを通じて広がる。

Fake news _____ itself through social media.

5. 彼の興味は写真から映画撮影に移っていった。

His interest _____ from photography to filmmaking.

6. あいつはいつも同じ奴らとつるんでいる。

He _____ out with the same guys all the time.

7. その運動が数千人の市民を動かし、政府への抗議に向かわせた。

The movement _____ thousands of citizens to protest against the government.

8. この考えは多くの研究者から支持を得てきた。

This idea has been _____ by many researchers.

➤ 下記の 形容詞または副詞 ＝英英・英日の語義が成立するように、空欄を埋めなさい。

1. o □□□□□□□ al = infrequent, sporadic「時折の、たまの」

2. in □□□□□□□□ = unassailable, sacrosanct「不可侵の」

3. in □□□□□□□□ = groundbreaking, inventive「革新的な」

4. pro □□□□□□□ = adept, expert「熟達した、堪能な」

5. t □□□□□□ ly = commonly, characteristically「通例、典型的に」

6. vo □□□□□□□ = avid, ardent「貪欲な、熱心な」

7. pro □□□□□ = productive「多作な」

8. a □□□□□ ly = probably, possibly「ほぼ確実に、おそらくは」

9. p □□□□□□ ly = discreetly, sensibly「慎重に、思慮深く」

10. p □□□□ ible = reasonable, likely「妥当と思われる、うなずける」

💬 Comprehension Check **True or False**

下の英文が本文の内容として正しい場合は T、間違っている場合は F を選びましょう。

1. Booksellers may find it difficult to decide the genre of Margaret Atwood's *The Handmaid's Tale*. (T / F)

2. Genre authors may use others' ideas, gimmicks, and styles. (T / F)

3. Fans of genre writers always want to read something new and innovative. (T / F)

4. The concept of genre does not go so well with poems as with novels. (T / F)

5. The real name of the author of *City of Glass* is Daniel Quinn. (T / F)

Comprehension Check **Multiple Choice**

本文の内容に照らして最も正しいものを a 〜 c の中から選んで○をつけなさい。

1. Which of the following is suggested by S. S. Van Dine's first rule for the crime writer?
   a. The mystery must not be so difficult as to prevent the reader from solving the mystery.
   b. The detective must not use clues unavailable to the reader to solve the mystery.
   c. Some clues should be obscure or concealed.

2. John Grisham earned much money by
   a. creating a new genre.
   b. reusing Robert Traver's idea.
   c. developing a breakthrough MacGuffin.

3. According to the author, writers of genre
   a. like to dress as their favourite characters at Worldcon.
   b. usually work with a team of assistants in order to publish many books.
   c. are generally not willing to try new genres.

4. Which of the following does NOT reflect the author's view?
   a. Writers should follow the rules for fiction created by a 'master' like Henry James.
   b. In terms of magic realist elements, *Midnight's Children* is closer to *Village of the Damned* than to *What Maisie Knew*.
   c. *Possession: A Romance* crosses over genres, and can also be included in 'high' literature.

5. Which of the following best describes *City of Glass*?

    a. It won an Edgar though it was not a crime novel at all.

    b. It is both conventional and unconventional as a detective story.

    c. It is old-fashioned and boring.

ACTIVE LEARNING for Discussion

1. 現在の日本で流行しているジャンル、すたれてしまったジャンルにはどのようなものがあるでしょうか。またそこにはどのような理由があると思いますか。ペアまたはグループで話し合ってみましょう。

2. 第14パラグラフ 'Genre, that is, is the magma in which literature finds its primal existence.' という表現で筆者は何を言おうとしているのでしょうか。本文に挙げられた例を基に考えてみましょう。また同じような例が思いつきますか。ペアまたはグループで話し合ってみましょう。

3. 本文に述べられているように、「ジャンル」の意味合いは立場によって変わってきます。読者にとって、作品を分類するジャンルの存在にはどのようなメリット、デメリットがありえるでしょうか。ペアまたはグループで話し合ってみましょう。

 読むならまずこの一冊

フィリップ・K・ディック『高い城の男』浅倉久志訳（ハヤカワ文庫）
「ＳＦ界のシェイクスピア」とも称されるディック。歴史改変ＳＦの本作は、奇想天外な展開もありつつ哲学的思索にも富み、「ジャンル小説」の枠に収まらない魅力がある。

CHAPTER 10

アレゴリー

Allegory

文学の最もしたたかな芸当は、あることを、全く別のことを言うことで述べることである。アレゴリーは直喩（「私の恋人は赤い赤い薔薇のよう」）および隠喩（「おお薔薇よ、汝は病めり」）に近いが、それらと異なって一回限りの技法あるいは装飾ではない。システムとして見るほうがより適切だろう。かなり長くなることもあるし、ときには作品全体に至ることもある（例えばスペンサーの叙事詩『妖精の女王』の一連の巻、第一は「神聖さ」をアレゴリー化し第二巻は「節制」云々のように）。ナラティヴ（バニヤンの『天路歴程』のように）もアレゴリーになりうる。その全体性から言ってアレゴリーは隠喩にはなりえない。それならばアレゴリーは一体どのようにしてその策を弄するのだろう？　そして文学はなぜそんなにもこの技法を好むのだろう？

 Pre-reading Vocabulary Check

日本語の意味に合う英文になるよう、次の中から適切なものを選びなさい。必要に応じて形を変えなさい。

> similes・enlighten・simultaneously・possession・unvarnished・
> sophisticated・obtrusive・digestible

1. この食べ物は赤ん坊には消化しにくい。
This food is not ＿＿＿＿＿＿＿＿ for babies.

2. その画家は憑依の暗いムードを紫の色であらわした。
The painter employed the color purple to express a dark mood for ＿＿＿＿＿＿＿.

3. 彼らは同時にしゃべりだした。
They began to talk ＿＿＿＿＿＿＿＿＿.

4. 彼のデザインはいつもとても洗練されている。
His designs are always very ＿＿＿＿＿＿＿＿.

5. 私はルソーの著作によって啓蒙されたのです。
I was ＿＿＿＿＿＿＿ by the works of Rousseau.

6. 私はその男性の差し出がましい態度に面食らった。
I was bewildered by the man's ＿＿＿＿＿＿ attitude.

7. 彼女はその絨毯の素朴な手触りが気に入った。
She liked the ＿＿＿＿＿＿＿ texture of the rug.

8. この種の直喩の用い方はまさにその作家特有のものだ。
This kind of use of ＿＿＿＿ is very unique to the writer.

Reading Passage

🔊 Audio 2-02

1 Plato uses allegory to clinch* his point   One of the earliest, and most vivid, allegories is that of 'the cave', in Plato's *Republic*. Socrates is talking to Glaucon, instructing him on the nature of knowledge, and the limits set on it by the human condition. 'Let me show in a *figure*,' he says, 'how far our nature is enlightened or unenlightened': 5

'Behold! human beings living in a underground den, which has a mouth open towards the light and reaching all along the den; here they have been from their childhood, and have their legs and necks chained so that they cannot move, and can only see before them, being prevented by the chains from turning round their heads. Above and behind them a fire is blazing 10 at a distance, and between the fire and the prisoners there is a raised way; and you will see, if you look, a low wall built along the way, like the screen which marionette players have in front of them, over which they show the puppets.'

This is not a fable* about unfortunate potholers* but an allegory of the sadly 15 handicapped way (as Plato saw it) that we benighted* humans will always know the real world.

2 But why doesn't Socrates just say it straight out? Why draw on a 'figure' to get the message across? Many reasons suggest* themselves. Not least, of course, his allegory beautifies. It can also be said to crystallize. And it makes 20 what he is saying memorable. Once read or heard, no one ever forgets that Platonic image*.

3 Modern thoughts about allegory   Serious dispute over the merits of allegory began with interpretation of the Bible in the nineteenth century, as its literal holy writ* wilted* in the face of science, rationalism and 25 Enlightenment scepticism*. Could a man survive for three days inside the intestines* of a whale, as we are told Jonah did, only to be spat up, good as new, on land? No. It's an allegory, of course, for the enslavement of the Israelites in the bowels of Egypt*.

4 Schopenhauer in *The Horrors and Absurdities of Religion* is eloquently 30 satirical on the subject of allegory. His essay takes the form of a dialogue – or quarrel – between Philalethes (who demands the truth, the whole truth, and nothing but the truth) and Demopheles, who argues that 'you've got to see that the needs of ordinary people have to be met in a way they can understand.' They have no greater need than religion, and allegory is the only way they can take it in:

> 'Religion is truth allegorically and mythically expressed, and so rendered attainable and digestible by mankind in general. Mankind couldn't possibly take it pure and unmixed, just as we can't breathe pure oxygen; we require an addition of four times its bulk in nitrogen. In plain language, the profound meaning, the high aim of life, can only be unfolded and presented to the masses* symbolically, because they are incapable of grasping it in its true signification.'

5 **'Philosophy,' he sagely observes, 'is not for everyone'.** Neither, of course, is economics. The financial catastrophe that ravaged the Western world in 2009* was conveyed 'allegorically and mythically' in terms the everyday victim could understand – such as 'credit crunch*', 'toxic loan*', 'double dip recession*'.

6 Written and pictorial allegory was at its most sophisticated in the medieval and Renaissance periods. It persists in modern literature as enriched texture rather than an obtrusive device. Allegory, at all periods, requires sophisticated readers capable of holding two very different kinds of truth simultaneously in their minds. Is Dorothea Brooke's the story of one remarkable (fictional) woman, or the story of a nineteenth-century (factual) Everywoman? We must maintain both hypotheses in a kind of tension when we read *Middlemarch*.

7 Not to perceive allegorical meanings is to blunder* into comical literalism, as did the *Country Life* reviewer of Kenneth Grahame's delightful anthropomorphic* allegory, *Wind in the Willows*, who complained that the depiction of Ratty (the amiable rodent* who loved 'messing about in boats*') was zoologically* inaccurate. True enough, but foolish.

8 **The allegorical twist in the tail** H. G. Wells' *The War of the Worlds*, a work thrown off by a young man in the 1890s, is among the most read of early science fiction romances. One reads it as a rattling* invasion yarn about bloodsucking aliens – inspired by the recent 'discovery' of canals on Mars*. But just once, in passing, Wells brushes his authorial finger across a button that transforms the whole work:

> 'And before we judge of [the Martians*] too harshly we must remember what ruthless and utter destruction our own species has wrought*, not

only upon animals, such as the vanished bison and the dodo*, but upon its 70
inferior races. The Tasmanians*, in spite of their human likeness, were
entirely swept out of existence in a war of extermination* waged* by
European immigrants, in the space of fifty years. Are we such apostles* of
mercy* as to complain if the Martians warred in the same spirit?'

9 The novel, the reader apprehends, allegorizes European colonialism* and 75
its genocides*. Sticking to the mid-1890s, is *Dr Jekyll and Mr Hyde* a Gothic
tale of demonic possession, or an allegory about the unconscious self that, in
Vienna, Freud was beginning to make sense of*? Is Oscar Wilde's *Dorian
Gray*, with his real self in the attic*, a fantasy, or an allegory of the
subterfuges* forced on the 'love that dare not speak its name'* in the 1890s? 80

10 Schopenhauer fondly believed that man would grow out of its allegorical
primitivism 'as out of his childhood clothes'. He was wrong. Ambiguity points
us to words meaning more than one thing. Allegory enlarges that double
meaning to whole texts. If you want naked, unvarnished, single truth, as
does Philalethes, don't go to literature. If you want many truths, compressed 85
into their full complexity, literature is exactly the place to go.

---

1 clinch：「まとめる」
fable：「寓話、たとえ話」
potholer：「洞窟探検家」
benighted：「暗愚な」
2 suggest：「思いつかせる」
Platonic image：「プラトン的イメージ」 ▶解説
3 writ：「文書、聖典」
wilt：「勢いを失う」
scepticism：「懐疑主義」
intestine：「腸」
the enslavement of the Israelites in the bowels of Egypt：「エジプト内部におけるイスラエル
人の奴隷化」 ▶解説
4 the masses：「大衆」
5 The financial catastrophe that ravaged the Western world in 2009：「2009年に西欧を襲っ
た経済危機」 ▶解説
credit crunch：「金融機関の貸し渋り」
toxic loan：「返還や利益の見込みのないまま行われる貸付」
double dip recession：「一度短期的に回復した後に再び落ち込む二段構えの景気後退、W字型不況」
7 blunder：「大失態をしでかす、つまずく」
anthropomorphic：「擬人化した」
rodent：「齧歯類動物」
messing about in boats：「ボートに乗ってぶらぶらすること」
zoologically：「動物学的に」

8 rattling：「厄介な」

the recent 'discovery' of canals on Mars：「近年の火星における運河の「発見」」　▶解説

Martian：「火星人」

wrought：「work の過去分詞」

dodo：「ドードー」インド洋のモーリシャス島などに生息していた飛べない鳥。白人入植者による乱獲などにより 17 世紀に絶滅した。

the Tasmanians：「タスマニア先住民」オーストラリア・タスマニア島に住んでいたが 19 世紀の白人による残虐な入植行為により絶滅した。

extermination：「根絶」

wage：「遂行する」

apostle：「使者」

mercy：「慈悲」

9 colonialism：「植民地主義」自国外の地域に侵入、経済的に開発して植民地とし、その経営・維持を通して覇権を得ようとする政策。

genocide：「大量殺戮」

the unconscious self that, in Vienna, Freud was beginning to make sense of：　▶解説

attic：「屋根裏」

subterfuge：「言い逃れ、ごまかし」

'love that dare not speak its name'：「「あえてその名をかたらぬ愛」」　▶解説

Post-reading Vocabulary Check

➤ 日本語の意味に合う英文になるよう、次の中から適切な 動詞 を選び、必要に応じて形を変えなさい。

> render・enrich・convey・stick・apprehend・maintain・prevent・persist

1. 彼は直ちに彼女がそこにいる理由を悟った。

He immediately _____ why she was there.

2. 彼の発言が事態をさらにややこしくした。

His remark _____ the situation more complicated.

3. 彼女はこの文字で何を伝えようとしたのだろうか。

What did she try to _____ to us by this letter?

4. 彼はその議題に会議の終わりになってもまだこだわっていた。

He still _____ to the subject at the very end of the meeting.

5. この家の維持にはとても金がかかります。

It costs us a lot to _____ this house.

6. 文学は我々の暮らしを非常に豊かなものにしてくれる。

Literature enormously _____ our lives.

7. この雑草の根は非常にしぶとい。

The root of this weed _____ very long.

8. 文法上の間違いを防ぐために辞書を使い倒しなさい。

Make the most of your dictionary in order to _____ grammatical errors.

➤ 下記の 形容詞または副詞 =英英・英日の語義が成立するように、空欄を埋めなさい。

1. v □□□□ = lively「あざやかな」

2. u □□□□□□□□□ = miserable「不運な、みじめな」

3. s □□□□□□□□ = ironic「風刺的な、皮肉な」

4. o □□□□□□□ = average, common「並みの、普通の」

5. r □□□□□□□□□ = astonishing, outstanding「傑出した、すばらしい」

6. r □□□□□□□ = cold-blooded, cruel「無慈悲な、残酷な」

7. i □□□□□□□ = menial, lower in status「劣った」

8. whole = e □□□□□ , full「全体の」

Comprehension Check　True or False

下の英文が本文の内容として正しい場合は T、間違っている場合は F を選びましょう。

1. The person instructing Glaucon with the allegory of 'the cave' is Plato.　　　(T / F)

2. Serious controversy over the significance of allegory in the nineteenth century was deeply concerned with the Bible.　　　(T / F)

3. It has been scientifically proved that Jonah, an existent Hebrew, actually survived for three days in the intestines of a whale.　　　(T / F)

4. Today, Kenneth Graham's *Wind in the Willows* is severely criticized for its inaccuracy in the depiction of animal life.　　　(T / F)

5. It is very advisable to read the literary work word for word and reach the only universal interpretation.　　　(T / F)

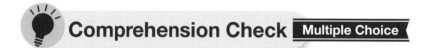

Comprehension Check　Multiple Choice

本文の内容に照らして最も正しいものを a 〜 c の中から選んで○をつけなさい。

1. Plato uses the allegory of 'the cave' to show that
   a. human beings' ability to know the world is quite limited.
   b. Socrates is an experienced potholer.
   c. leading a primitive life is crucial to human beings.

2. Which of the following is true about *Wind in the Willows*?
   a. It was published as an introductory text of zoology.
   b. The *Country Life* reviewer 'blundered into comical literalism' because the person expected it to be a botanical work judging from the title.
   c. Kenneth Grahame depicted the animals as if they were human beings.

3. Which of the following is true about H. G. Wells and *The War of the Worlds*?
   a. Wells was really afraid of the aliens' attack.
   b. *The War of the Worlds* actually criticizes human beings' greed and cruelty.
   c. The novel shows Wells' obsession with the idea of becoming a Martian.

4. *Dr Jekyll and Mr Hyde* can be related to Sigmund Freud if
   a. it is read as a biography of Freud.
   b. it is interpreted psychoanalytically.
   c. the readers have enough knowledge about European colonialism at that time.

5. Oscar Wilde's *Dorian Gray* can be read as an allegory of the subterfuges forced on the 'love that dare not speak in its name' because

   a. everybody was practicing that kind of love when it was published.

   b. there was great prejudice against male homosexuality in the 1890s.

   c. Wilde was one of the fierce attackers of homosexuality.

 ACTIVE LEARNING for Discussion

1. 今まで読んだことのある小説や物語などを思い出して、アレゴリーと判断できるものにはどのようなものがあるか、ペアまたはグループで話し合ってみましょう。

2. 第5パラグラフ、リーマン・ショック時に用いられた 'credit crunch', 'toxic loan', 'double dip recession' などの語が「平凡な、一般の（everyday）」被害者たちが理解できる用語であるというのはなぜでしょうか。ペアまたはグループで話し合ってみましょう。

3. 第7パラグラフ、Kenneth Grahame が *Wind in the Willows* で用いているとされる「擬人法」ですが、この技法にはどのような効果があると思いますか。ペアまたはグループで話し合ってみましょう。

 読むならまずこの一冊

アーサー・ミラー『るつぼ』（ハヤカワ演劇文庫など）
20世紀米国を代表する劇作家アーサー・ミラーが、17世紀ニューイングランドで実際に起こった魔女狩りに材を得ながら、1950年代米国の赤狩りを鋭く批判するこの戯曲では、アレゴリーの効果をよく確認できるだろう。

CHAPTER 11

Metafiction

メタフィクション

メタフィクションは、自分自身が何かの模倣であることを意識した上で、その自意識に喜んで身を任せる物語である。作品の集積が時とともに増大していくにつれ、文学はより自意識的になり、オリジナリティを見出すことはますます難しくなってきている。文学の歴史という建物を鉄球で取り壊してしまうことはできないのだ。それどころか作品はいっそう速度を増して、容赦なく積み重なっていく。19 世紀半ばのディケンズの時代には、一年に発表される小説の数は千にも満たなかった。ところが 21 世紀の現在では、一万を下回る年はほとんどない。そしてその一万の作品が、エコー室で音が反響するように、互いに影響を与えあっているのである。

 ## Pre-reading Vocabulary Check

日本語の意味に合う英文になるよう、次の中から適切なものを選びなさい。必要に応じて形を変えなさい。

tribute ・ adaptations ・ use up ・ perspective ・ detect ・ standardize ・ playful ・ digress

1. 彼女はグローバルな視点からその問題を考える必要性を訴えた。
She stressed the need to see the issue from a global _____.

2. SAT はアメリカの大学入学選考で広く使われている標準テストである。
The SAT is a _____ test widely used for college admissions in the United States.

3. 私はすべての力を使い果たしてしまった。
I have _____ all of my energy.

4. 町の人々はその火事で死んだ消防士たちに敬意を表した。
The town paid _____ to the firefighters who died in the fire.

5. ちょっとだけ話は脱線しますが、来週は授業がないということを再度お伝えしておきます。
To _____ for a moment, I'd like to remind you that there will be no class next week.

6. シェイクスピアの戯曲にはたくさんの映画版がある。
There are a lot of film _____ of Shakespeare's plays.

7. その検査は病気を早期に発見することを目的としている。
The test is designed to _____ the disease early.

8. 彼はふざけているような表情を浮かべていた。
He had a _____ expression on his face.

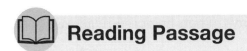 **Reading Passage**

Audio 2-03

1 **Is all fiction metafiction?** The term 'metafiction' is of recent origin – no more than four decades old. But with hindsight*, one can detect metafictional elements in the earliest works of literature. *Don Quixote*, for example, is an 'anti-romance*'. The melancholy knight, with his cardboard armour* and comic misapprehensions* of chivalry*, is Cervantes' playful 5 metafictional joust* with heroic works such as *The Song of the Cid*, and innumerable medieval romances of knight errantry*.

2 Literary parody* (e.g. Henry Fielding's *Shamela*, a hilarious take-off* of Samuel Richardson's *Pamela*) is one standardized form of metafiction. Homage* fiction (e.g. Michael Cunningham's *The Hours* – a tribute to 10 Virginia Woolf's *Mrs Dalloway*) is another, as is mock-epic* (e.g. Alexander Pope's *The Rape of the Lock*). A fourth kind of metafiction is the 'knowing variation on a folkloric* theme', such as J. M. Coetzee's *Foe* (there is another castaway*, a woman, on Robinson Crusoe's island – an acquaintance of a novelist called Daniel Foe). None of these works could themselves work 15 without other literature of whose existence they constantly remind the reader.

3 Metafiction is acutely aware of other fiction but also, characteristically*, elaborately self-aware as well. It typically indulges a 'narcissism*'– a 'look what I am doing' signal to the reader. Self-referentiality* is raised to the 20 status of an extended joke in a pioneer text in the high-metafiction canon*, Laurence Sterne's *Tristram Shandy*. At one sublimely* comic moment, well into the book, the narrator, Tristram, who has set out (like a horde* of other 'life writers*') to chronicle his whole 'Life and Opinions', discovers that the task he has set himself is impossible. His life is accumulating faster than he 25 can write it down. The narrator's need to digress (describe situations, events, circumstances) hinders the need to progress. He will never catch up with* himself. He's the sorcerer's apprentice*, with no sorcerer to rescue him. Metafiction typically blends into metanarrative* in this Shandyan way.

4 Of course novelists, like other narrators (those in film, for example, who 30 have only two hours to work with), have developed strategies for circumventing* the Tristram quandary* – without troubling the reader on the subject. But Sterne *intends* to trouble the reader: it's the basic joke. 'My

next trick is impossible', as the conjuror* says. Then he goes ahead and does
35 it.

5 One could go so far as to* suggest that all fiction is metafictional to some
degree. If you know you are writing a novel, you will also know you are
working in the shadow of other novels. The novel can never be entirely novel.
There are writers in the modern period – as the body of literature has
40 multiplied unprecedentedly – who have used this fact, making generic
impossibility their métier*, or angle.

6 Donald Barthelme (1931–89) is one such metafictional virtuoso*. Best
known among his novels (or 'anti-novels') is *Snow White* (1967), a literary
fantasia on Disney's cartoon of the original German fairy story. Barthelme's
45 Snow White (the story begins with a corporeal inventory of her 'beauty
spots'*– including a fine one on her buttock) misconducts* herself
disgracefully* with her dwarfs* in the shower.

7 **Metafiction and originality**   Metafiction, one may say, focuses on the
perennial* literary problem – particularly troublesome for the modern writer
50 – of how to achieve originality within a larger, inescapable unoriginality. All
the literary space is occupied, all the stories used up. What can a writer do
but chew the gum other writers have left behind them?

8 One solution is to go back to those old stories and do them again – but
differently, with modern inflections* and twists. Chew the old gum
55 differently. This literary recidivism* has produced a rich crop, in recent
years, of so called post-Victorian Victorian novels. It represents one of the
more popular veins of contemporary metafiction, and would seem to have
plenty of juice left in it.

9 The point of origin is a novel by Robert Graves, *The Real David
60 Copperfield* (1933). Graves' novel mischievously switches perspective,
narrating Dickens' version from a different angle. It introduces 'grown-up'
elements – no 'happy ever after' for the hero with his Agnes, for example; his
sexual desires are much more complex than those of Dickens' David (it is he,
not Steerforth, who lusts after L'il Emily).

65 **10** Following Graves, there has been a profusion of* alternative angle
PVVNs*– *Wuthering Heights* from the point of view of Nelly Dean, *Jane Eyre*
from the point of view of Bertha Mason (e.g. Jean Rhys' *Wide Sargasso Sea*).
This genre has been hugely boosted by the millions' strong audience which
television has recruited for Victorian period serial* dramatisation. Andrew

Davies' adaptation of George Eliot's *Middlemarch* made that novel a Number 70
One paperback bestseller in 1994. Trollope, Dickens, and Mrs Gaskell have
all enjoyed a similar posthumous* success. It creates a vibrant reciprocity*.
The novel – say *Vanity Fair*, or Trollope's *The Way We Live Now*, is televised,
then it is extensively read (often by reading groups – a fascinating modern
phenomenon) and then it slips on to the prescribed reading of schools and 75
universities. The author lives again.

11 A super-seller in the neo-Victorian genre is George MacDonald Fraser's
'Flashman' series, which follows the outrageous career of the 'cad*' villain in
Tom Brown's Schooldays through a dozen volumes. A *ne plus ultra** among
PVVNs is Jasper Fforde's burlesque* 'Thursday Next' series. In one of the 80
books (*The Well of Lost Plots*), the central characters of *Wuthering Heights*
appear as plaintiffs* before a tribunal* of 'jurisfiction*' to establish which of
them has legal ownership of their narrative*. On a more serious plane are
novels like A. S. Byatt's Booker Prize-winning* *Possession*, John Fowles' *The
French Lieutenant's Woman* and Sarah Waters' *Fingersmith*, which do 85
Victorian fiction a century after the era is dead and gone. As the great corpus
of literature grows, metafiction – novels about novels – will, to a certainty,
grow too. Who knows, one day it may be the only kind of fiction available.

---

1 with hindsight：「あと知恵で、あとから考えてみると」
anti-romance：「反ロマンス」'romance' はここでは中世に数多く書かれた騎士道物語のこと。
cardboard armour：「名ばかりの粗末な鎧」'cardboard' は「厚紙製の」という意味だが、ここでは比喩的に用いられている。
misapprehension：「考え違い」
chivalry：「騎士道精神」
joust：「一騎打ち、戦い」
errantry：「（修行のための）諸国遍歴」
2 parody：「パロディ」▶解説
hilarious take-off：「滑稽な物まね」
homage：「オマージュ、敬意」▶解説
mock-epic：「擬似英雄詩」▶解説／Chapter 4 Epic
folkloric：「民間伝承の」
castaway：「難破した人」
3 characteristically：「特色として、特質上」
narcissism：「自己愛、ナルシシズム」▶解説
self-referentiality：「自己言及性」▶解説
the high-metafiction canon：「主流とされる高尚なメタフィクションのキャノン」▶ Chapter 8 The Canon
sublimely：「きわめて」
horde：「群れ、多数」
life writers：18世紀のイギリスで流行していた、自伝や回想録の形式で自らの人生やそこから得た教訓（'life and opinions'）などを語る作家たちのこと。

catch up with：「～に追いつく」

sorcerer's apprentice：「魔法使いの見習い」

metanarrative：「メタナラティヴ」　▶解説

4 circumvent：「回避する」

quandary：「窮地、板挟み」

conjuror：「奇術師」

5 go so far as to：「～するまでに至る」

métier：「技巧」

6 virtuoso：「名手」

corporeal inventory of her 'beauty spots'：「彼女のほくろの形を一覧にしたもの」

misconduct：「(性的な) 不品行をはたらく」

disgracefully：「不名誉にも」

dwarf：「小びと」

7 perennial：「長年続く」

8 inflection：「屈折、変化」

recidivism：「再犯、常習的犯行」

10 a profusion of：「おびただしい量の」

PVVNs：post-Victorian Victorian novels の頭文字を取ったもの

serial：「続きものの、連載の」

posthumous：「死後の」

vibrant reciprocity：「刺激的な相互作用」

11 cad：「不良の男」

ne plus ultra：「極限、極地」

burlesque：「バーレスク、戯作」　▶解説

plaintiff：「原告」

tribunal：「判事席」

jurisfiction：「小説裁判」 'jurisdiction'（裁判権）と 'fiction'（小説）を組み合わせた造語。

legal ownership of their narrative：「物語の法的所有権」　▶ Chapter 3 Narrative / Story

Booker Prize：「ブッカー賞」　▶解説

Post-reading Vocabulary Check

➤ 日本語の意味に合う英文になるよう、次の中から適切な 動詞 を選び、必要に応じて形を変えなさい。

indulge・multiply・accumulate・hinder・occupy・blend・lust・trouble

1. 何も言わずに黙っていることはしばしば問題を増大させる。
Silence often _____ the problem.

2. ご面倒をおかけしてすみませんが、車を移動していただけませんか。
I'm sorry to _____ you, but could you move your car?

3. 座席はすべてふさがっていた。
The seats are all _____ .

4. 彼は群衆に溶け込もうとした。
He tried to _____ into the crowd.

5. 現在の政治状況は経済の成長を妨げている。
The current political situation _____ economic growth.

6. 雪が屋根に積もってきている。
Snow is _____ on the roof.

7. 遺産のおかげで彼は芸術への情熱をほしいままにできた。
The inheritance enabled him to _____ his passion for art.

8. 彼は高校時代から権力を強く欲していた。
He has _____ for power since his high school days.

➤ 下記の 名詞、形容詞または副詞 ＝英英・英日の語義が成立するように、空欄を埋めなさい。

1. in ⬜⬜⬜⬜⬜ able = too many to be counted, countless「無数の」

2. ac ⬜⬜⬜⬜⬜⬜⬜ ce = colleague, associate, friend「知人」

3. ela ⬜⬜⬜⬜⬜ ly = in a detailed or complicated way「入念に」

4. unprecedented = not known or experienced before, new, ori ⬜⬜⬜⬜⬜「先例のない」

5. g ⬜⬜⬜⬜⬜ c = common, overall, general「一般的な」

6. m ⬜⬜⬜⬜⬜⬜ vously = playfully「いたずらっぽく」

7. ou ⬜⬜⬜⬜⬜ us = very unusual, very shocking「常軌を逸した」

8. vi ⬜⬜⬜⬜⬜ = the main bad character in a story, a wicked person「悪役」

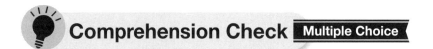

Comprehension Check True or False

下の英文が本文の内容として正しい場合は T、間違っている場合は F を選びましょう。

1. The first metafiction was written about forty years ago.　　　　　　(T / F)

2. *Don Quixote* is an example of a novel which is acutely aware of other literature.

　　　　　　　　　　　　　　　　　　　　　　　　　　　　　　　(T / F)

3. The author uses the word 'narcissism' (l. 19) to describe metafiction's self-referential tendency.　　　　　　　　　　　　　　　　　　　　　　(T / F)

4. The authors of contemporary metafiction give up the idea of originality because all the stories are used up.　　　　　　　　　　　　　　　　　　(T / F)

5. The author suggests that metafiction will continue developing in the future. (T / F)

Comprehension Check Multiple Choice

本文の内容に照らして最も正しいものを a ～ c の中から選んで○をつけなさい。

1. Which of the following is NOT an example of metafiction?
   a. Henry Fielding's *Shamela*
   b. Virginia Woolf's *Mrs Dalloway*
   c. J. M. Coetzee's *Foe*

2. Which of the following is true about *Tristram Shandy*?
   a. It is full of self-referential jokes.
   b. It is written in the same way as other works of 'life writers'.
   c. Sterne tries to avoid digressing.

3. By the phrase 'chew the old gum differently' (ll. 54-55), the author refers to
   a. the impossibility of writing metafiction.
   b. the need to make literature more popular.
   c. a way to achieve originality.

4. Which of the following is NOT true about the post-Victorian Victorian novels?
   a. They often switch the point of view of the story.
   b. They are popular, but already used up.
   c. Their readers include the audience of TV adaptations of Victorian fiction.

5. The author suggests that metafiction

    a. gives the reader a way to get away from narcissism.

    b. is basically a joke.

    c. can make older novels popular once again.

 ACTIVE LEARNING for Discussion

1. 本文中にはたくさんのメタフィクションが挙げられています。巻末の「作家・（登場）人物・作品リスト」を参照してそれぞれの作品について知り、特に興味を持った作品についてより詳しく調べてみましょう。

2. 現代日本の小説、映画、漫画、アニメにもメタフィクションと呼べる作品は数多くあります。自分の知っている例を取り上げて、その作品におけるメタフィクション的要素がどのようなものでどのような効果を発揮しているかを具体的に考え、ペアまたはグループで話し合ってみましょう。

3. 本文中では、メタフィクションという概念の紹介を通じて、現代においてオリジナリティとはどういうものでありりうるかが考察されています。ここで述べられているオリジナリティに対する考え方について、あなたはどう思いますか。自分の考えをまとめ、ペアまたはグループで話し合ってみましょう。

 読むならまずこの一冊

カート・ヴォネガット『スローターハウス５』伊藤典夫訳（ハヤカワ文庫）

メタフィクションが「語ることに対する自意識とためらい」の表現でもあるならば、語らねばならないがどうしても語りにくい出来事を語るとき、メタフィクションを通じて「語れなさ」自体を主題にすることができる。語らねばならないが語りにくい出来事。その最たるものがたとえば「戦争体験」ではないだろうか。この作品は、第二次世界大戦従軍中に人類史上未曾有の爆撃を経験した著者による、「戦争を語ること」についての切実なメタフィクションである。

CHAPTER 12

構造主義
Structuralism

　言語学や人類学の分野で発展した構造主義は、やがて文学批評にも応用されるようになった。文学にとって「構造」とは何か？　文学を文学たらしめる不変の「構造」は存在するのだろうか？

　「ダルグリッシュなら構造主義についてどう考えるか、訊ねられたんです——それともポスト構造主義だったかしら？」とＰ・Ｄ・ジェイムズ（P. D. James）は考え込む。「私はこう答えました。彼は夜な夜な考えた挙句、あんなのは戯言だという結論に達したでしょう」。ジェイムズ女男爵（イギリスでもっとも著名な推理小説家）は思い違いをしている。構造主義／ポスト構造主義の提示した問題（文学に内在する型についての議論）は、アダム・ダルグリッシュ（Adam Dalgliesh）警部が時間をかけて検討する価値のあるものだ。もしかしたら、それによって彼の詩も深みが増すかもしれないのだ。

 Pre-reading Vocabulary Check

日本語の意味に合う英文になるよう、次の中から適切なものを選びなさい。必要に応じて形を変えなさい。

> get round・profane・run counter・abstract・parables・framework・
> treacherous・singularity

1. 一神教とは神の唯一性を信じるものである。
   Monotheism is the belief in the _____ of the divine.

2. 財政への影響に対処するため、現行法の枠内で即座の処置がとられねばならない。
   Immediate steps must be taken to address the financial impact within the _____ of existing law.

3. この本の題名は不誠実で誤解を招く。
   The title of this book is _____ and misleading.

4. いくつかの楽器は卑俗あるいは世俗的とみなされており、ミサでは使用できない。
   Some musical instruments are regarded as _____ or secular, and cannot be used at Mass.

5. 我々人間は個別から普遍を抽象する能力を有している。
   We humans have the ability to _____ the universal from the particular.

6. チームを去るという彼女の決断は皆の予想に反していた。
   Her decision to leave the team _____ to everyone's expectations.

7. どのようにすれば地球環境の危機を乗り越えらえるかについては長年議論がなされてきた。
   There have been longstanding debates over how we can _____ the ecological crisis.

8. 放蕩息子の物語は新約聖書の中でもっとも有名なたとえ話の一つである。
   The story of the prodigal son is one of the most famous _____ in the New Testament.

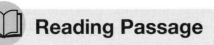 **Reading Passage**

Audio 2-04

1 Can literature be a 'structure'? Literature is linear – lines. Lines on a page, in script; or pixelated*, left to right, on a screen; or heard over two hours in a theatre. Yet we routinely talk of a novel, a play or a poem spatially, with words like 'form', or 'structure'. Writers, on their side, often 'see' their work spatially. Wordsworth airily pictures his autobiographical 5 poem *The Prelude* as the 'ante-chapel*' to the 'cathedral' that will be the larger structure (never completed), *The Excursion*. So, too, Henry James' 'house of fiction' – all those millions of lines coming together as one three-dimensional edifice: as solid as James' mansion in Rye*.

2 So we *read* a novel as lines on the page and simultaneously *see* it as one 10 might see a painting or a sculpture. There are, however, treacherous false analogies lurking in that comparison.

3 If a husband and wife, on holiday in France, look at the Venus de Milo* in the Louvre*, the man (as surveys confirm) will probably look at the statue's breasts first and the woman will first look at the face. If the couple have both 15 brought the same book with them to read (say *The Da Vinci Code* – to keep up the Louvre theme), they will, both of them, start at page 1 and work through to page 2. Linearly. Mr Tourist will not start at page 60 and work back and forwards, and Mrs Tourist at page 90.

4 In an important sense it is the reader who, following the long line of a 20 literary text, 'makes' it; or, put another way, makes sense of it; like Dalgliesh, or Sherlock Holmes, assembling their 'clues' into a narrative. Works of literature are not there, fully made – even the shortest, most imagistic* works, which can be gulped down in a single eye bite*.

5 The reader's contribution The work of Literature is, largely, the 25 reader's job. To read is to construct: investing black marks on a white surface with meaning and, as one goes on, shape. The sculptor (unless they're very modern) doesn't give you a square block of marble and a set of chisels and tell you there's an interesting object somewhere inside. Authors routinely do just that. 30

6 Structuralism is unusually good at explaining itself to newcomers. Jonathan Culler (its high priest*) offers an illuminating parable. If, while strolling through a grassy meadow, I happen on a spherical stone and kick it between a couple of logs that happen to be nearby, what does it mean? Nothing. Just that I wanted to swing my leg. 35

7 Supposing, on a pitch at Wembley*, David Beckham shoots the ball into the net between the opposition uprights*. What gives his kick the meaning 'goal'? Not the grass, not the wooden uprights, not the netting, not the spheroid*, not Beckham's genius left foot, but the rules of association football. If Beckham picked up the soccer ball and ran with it through the posts, that would be a foul. But why, a couple of miles away, might it be a 'try'?

8 It is the 'structuration*' – the rules and all the invisible frameworks around these triumphs on the field – that construct the meaning.

9 Structuralism is a very exhilarating theory. When it burst on to the Anglo-American critical scene in the early 1960s, there was a sense of excitement: a 'Eureka!*' moment.

10 The most vivacious of the crew, Roland Barthes, when structuralism was *le dernier cri**, wrote a sparkling essay on, of all things un-French, 'Steak and Chips*'. When we sink our teeth into that particular dish, he lyricized*, we are not merely ingesting flesh: 'Steak is part of the same sanguine* mythology as wine. It is the heart of meat, it is meat in its pure state; and whoever partakes of it assimilates a bull-like strength.' It is, in a sense, a communion act – sacred. But while steak (the majestic Texan 32 oz T-bone, for example) confers national glamour, chips, Barthes suggests, are nostalgic and patriotic (french fries).

11 Problems   It's heady* stuff. But there are a number of problems with structuralism, when applied to literature, which render it if not Dalglieshian nonsense, then not quite the perfect Cinderella-shoe fit* one would like.

12 The theory of structuralism was developed initially in social anthropology to explain such things as gift exchange, totemism*, and the distinction between 'sacred' and 'profane' objects – the communion wafer* and a McVitie's* chocolate digestive, for example. Texts, or literary genres, are harder to work with, as Barthes found when he moved from edibles like steak and chips to literary narratives.

13 A second issue is structuralism's immateriality*. This is both a useful and a problematic aspect of the theory. Its usefulness is that it helps us get round the following awkwardness: if my Victorian ancestor is reading, in 1872, the first four-volume edition of *Middlemarch* and I, 140 years later, am reading the Penguin Classic*, are we reading the same novel? Yes, says the structuralist (a beefsteak is a beefsteak is a beefsteak*). But common sense (and historicist/new historicist* thinking) argues that I and my great-grandad are having very different experiences.

14 This immateriality links to a third objection. Namely that structuralism is ahistorical*. It abstracts literature from all its accidents of time and place.

This runs counter to common sense, which tells us that *Middlemarch* was a different kettle of fish* for a middle-class Victorian lady in 1874 from what it is for a twelfth-grader* or A-level student* today. Do the structures of Eliot's novel buckle and change – like Dali watches* – with the passing of time?

15 The most forceful objection is that structuralism is essentially 80 authoritarian in implying there is singularity, not multiplicity, in the meanings we find in any one work of literature, and that singularity is located in the work (or the author's 'art'), not our response. A work of literature, closely examined, can no more have two structures than the person examining it can have two backbones. 85

---

1 pixelated：「（低い解像度で）表示される」
ante-chapel：「（教会の）前室」
Rye：「ライ」英国イースト・サセックス州の町。
3 Venus de Milo：「ミロのヴィーナス」古代ギリシアで作られた女性像。
the Louvre：「ルーヴル美術館」
4 imagistic：「イマジスト的な」▶解説
can be gulped down in a single eye bite：「一目で飲みこめる」一目で読めるくらい短いことを表す。
6 high priest：「（主義・運動の）主導者、主唱者」
7 Wembley：「ウェンブリー・スタジアム」イングランドのサッカーチーム、マンチェスター・ユナイテッドの本拠地。
the opposition uprights：「敵陣のゴールポスト」
spheroid：「回転楕円体」ただし通常サッカーボールは球体（sphere）。
8 structuration：「構造化」
9 Eureka!：「見つけた！」を意味する古代ギリシア語。▶解説
10 *le dernier cri*：「最新流行」フランス語
steak and chips：「ステーキ・アンド・チップス」チップスはフライド・ポテト（フレンチ・フライ）を指す。
lyricize：「抒情的に述べる」
sanguine：「血液の」
11 heady：「興奮させる、酔わせる」
the perfect Cinderella-shoe fit：「シンデレラの靴のようにぴったりフィットするもの」
12 totemism：「トーテム崇拝」▶解説
communion wafer：「聖体拝領用の聖餅」
McVitie's：「マクヴィティ」ダイジェスティブ（全粒粉）ビスケットで有名な英国の会社。
13 immateriality：「非物質性」
the Penguin Classic：「ペンギン・クラシックス版」古典的作品を出版するペンギン・ブックス社のシリーズ。
a beefsteak is a beefsteak is a beefsteak：「ビーフステーキはビーフステーキでビーフステーキだ」▶解説
historicist/new historicist：「歴史主義／新歴史主義の」▶ Chapter 14 New Historicism
14 ahistorical：「非歴史的」
a different kettle of fish：「全くの別物」
twelfth-grader：「12 年生」日本の高校 3 年生にあたる。
A-level student：「A レベル（大学進学資格）取得を目指す学生」
Dali watches：サルバドール・ダリ（Salvador Dalí, 1904–89）の絵画に描かれる歪んだ時計を指す。

Post-reading Vocabulary Check

➤ 日本語の意味に合う英文になるよう、次の中から適切な 動詞 を選び、必要に応じて形を変えなさい。

> invest・lurk・assemble・buckle・partake・render・ingest・confer

1. 彼は一人きりでパンと水を摂った。
He _____ of bread and water in solitude.

2. 込み入った叙述スタイルが物語に悪夢的性質を付与している。
The convoluted narrative style _____ the story with a nightmarish quality.

3. その作家の手紙は一冊の本にまとめられた。
The writer's letters were _____ into a book.

4. この地域のコウモリの体内に新種のウィルスが潜んでいることがわかった。
New viruses have been found _____ in bats in this area.

5. 大量の海鳥がプラスチック摂取によって死んでいる。
A large number of seabirds are killed by _____ plastic.

6. 容赦ない熱さのせいで道が歪んでしまった。
The road _____ under the relentless heat.

7. 制服が力と威厳を授けてくれると彼らは信じている。
They believe that the uniform _____ power and dignity.

8. 彼女の忘れがたい演技がその映画を古典的名作にした。
Her unforgettable performance _____ the film a classic.

➤ 下記の 形容詞または副詞 ＝英英・英日の語義が成立するように、空欄を埋めなさい。

1. r □□□□□□ ly = customarily, regularly「日常的に、いつも決まって」

2. l □□□□ ly = mostly, chiefly「大部分は、主に」

3. i □□□□□□□□ ing = enlightening, clarifying「啓蒙的な、明らかにする」

4. e □□□□□□□ ing = exciting, thrilling「気持ちを盛り上げる、うきうきさせる」

5. v □□□□□□□ = lively, energetic「快活な、活発な」

6. majestic = g □□□□ , magnificent「荘厳な、堂々とした」

7. p □□□□□□□ ic = troublesome, awkward「問題含みの、厄介な」

8. f □□□ ful = powerful, convincing「強力な、説得力のある」

9. a □□□□□□□□ ian = favouring submission to authority「権威主義的な」

Comprehension Check — True or False

下の英文が本文の内容として正しい場合は T、間違っている場合は F を選びましょう。

1. People often use spatial vocabulary to discuss literature. (T / F)

2. Reading the shortest works of literature is a very different experience from seeing a sculpture. (T / F)

3. The author thinks that it is the reader who gives shape to a work of literature. (T / F)

4. If you kick a round object between two vertical poles, it invariably means a 'goal'. (T / F)

5. Structuralism thinks that a literary work can have only one structure which produces its meanings. (T / F)

Comprehension Check — Multiple Choice

本文の内容に照らして最も正しいものを a 〜 c の中から選んで○をつけなさい。

1. Which of the following describes a structuralist idea?
   a. Lines are the main component of literature.
   b. Works of literature are not there, fully made.
   c. The structure of a work of literature is not affected by time and place.

2. According to structuralism, meaning is constructed by
   a. the reader.
   b. common sense.
   c. structuration.

3. The author suggests that Roland Barthes' essay is
   a. nonsensical.
   b. lyrically written and enchanting.
   c. not a good example of structuralism.

4. 'Structuralism's immateriality' (l. 66) implies an idea that
   a. the material form of a literary work is irrelevant to its structure.
   b. one cannot have the same experience as their Victorian ancestor.
   c. literary works undergo historical changes.

5. The author argues that the weakest point of structuralism is that

    a. it goes against common sense.

    b. it denies the possibility that meanings of literary works change depending on who reads them, when and where.

    c. it is not good at dealing with texts.

 ## ACTIVE LEARNING for Discussion

1. Structuralism における 'structure' とは結局どのようなものを指しているのでしょうか。本文から読み取れることをペアまたはグループで話し合ってみましょう。

2. 本文では何が（誰が）文学作品の意味を構築するのかについて論じられています。あなたは意味構築で重要な役割を果たすのは何だと考えますか。ペアまたはグループで話し合ってみましょう。

3. 第 13-14 パラグラフの「140 年前の小説の出版当時の読者と現代の読者とでは、同じ小説を読んでいる、あるいは同じ経験をしていると言えるのか？」という疑問について、どう考えますか。ペアまたはグループで話し合ってみましょう。

 ## 読むならまずこの一冊

ミロラド・パヴィチ『ハザール事典──夢の狩人たちの物語』[男性版]、[女性版] 工藤幸雄訳（創元ライブラリ）
小説は前から後ろに読み進めるものという常識を覆す作品。文学作品の形式や構造の意義を改めて考えてみよう。

CHAPTER 13

脱構築

Deconstruction

フランスの哲学者ジャック・デリダ（Jacques Derrida）が提唱した脱構築は文学批評にも影響を及ぼし、20世紀後半の「理論」隆盛の礎を築いて文学批評の様相を一変させた。いっぽうで、それまでの文学批評を土台から崩してしまうように思われた脱構築は大きな反発も引き起こしてきた。

「私自身、脱構築を少々嗜んでいるんだが、これがなかなかエキサイティングでね。今や知的スリルを味わうための最後の手段だよ。木の枝に座りながら、その枝をギコギコ切っている感じなんだ」とモリス・ザップ（Morris Zapp）は言う。アメリカの批評家スタンリー・フィッシュをモデルにしたとされる、デイヴィッド・ロッジ（David Lodge）の小説『小さな世界』（*Small World*）の登場人物だ。過去40年以上、脱構築ほど広く誤解されてきた批評概念はほとんどない。文学批評がおかしくなったことを示す事例として真っ先に槍玉に挙げられてもきた。読書家は誰であれこの概念に慣れ親しむ必要があるのか、それともアカデミックな議論の中に閉じ込めておくべきなのか？

 ## Pre-reading Vocabulary Check

日本語の意味に合う英文になるよう、次の中から適切なものを選びなさい。必要に応じて形を変えなさい。

> involve・deride・so much so that・immigrant・scope・doctrine・
> in the wake of・faculty

1. 脱構築以降、どんな文学批評が可能だろうか。

What sort of literary criticism is possible _____ deconstruction?

2. ジョゼフ・コンラッドはポーランドからの移民だった。

Joseph Conrad was a Polish _____.

3. イェール大学の教員の何人かは脱構築者とみなされていた。

Several members of the Yale _____ were viewed as deconstructionists.

4. あなたは議論の範囲を絞り込む必要がある。

You need to narrow down the _____ of your discussion.

5. 誰も馬鹿だとあざけられたくはない。

Nobody wants to be _____ as a fool.

6. 脱構築には破壊と構築の両方がともなう。

Deconstruction _____ both destruction and construction.

7. ジャック・ラカンの理論は難しい。あまりに難しいのでしばしば読者を途方に暮れさせる。

Jacques Lacan's theories are difficult to understand. _____ they often leave the reader at a loss.

8. その教理の根拠は聖書にはない。

The bible affords no ground for the _____.

Reading Passage

Audio 2-05

1 Its arrival on the scene   The emergence of deconstruction in the English-speaking world can be precisely dated. It happened on 21 October 1966, when Jacques Derrida gave his lecture '*La Structure, le signe et le jeu dans le discours des sciences humaines* *' at the International Colloquium on
5 Critical Languages and the Sciences of Man*, at Johns Hopkins University in Baltimore.

2 Derrida had travelled from France with Roland Barthes and Jacques Lacan, two other foundational figures in the rise to dominance of what would thereafter be called (misleadingly) 'theory*'. Initially derided as 'higher
10 Froggy nonsense*', the new approach took off like wildfire among the younger American faculty. So much so that the high priest of deconstruction, Jacques Derrida, could assert in the 1980s, 'America *is* Deconstruction.'

3 As young *doctrinaires** progressed upward through the academic ranks, it became orthodoxy* — and to the non-academic world, scandal. The essential
15 tenet* of deconstruction, as amusingly outlined in David Lodge's Zappism* above, is that any encounter with literature involves arbitrarily constructing meaning, then promptly erasing that meaning, only to go through the process again with the reassembled text. There is no finality; every literary text is inherently indeterminate*. The only conclusion, depressingly, is what the
20 deconstructionists call 'aporia': total dead end, out of which there is no way forward, or back.

4 A pessimistic doctrine?   Why, if the journey is so pointless, go on with it? At least when Penelope wove (by day) and unwove (by night) her absent husband's burial shroud, there was a reason. Why construct and deconstruct
25 *Hamlet*, simply to go through the process again – ad infinitum*?

5 Because, deconstruction explains, the making of meanings, however arbitrary, is the only lifeline we shall ever have across the abyss of unmeaningness. Writing literature (*écriture**) is an analogous activity. Deconstruction pictures authors and readers as like the Flying Wallendas*
30 in their high-wire act across the Grand Canyon. Why do it? Because it's walk the quivering high wire or plummet into the gulf of unmeaning below.

6 Deconstruction involved two quite opposite moves in its heyday (roughly the mid-1960s to the 1980s). One was a broadening of scope with a generous gulp of European (principally French) philosophy. At the same time, as it coalesced into a school in the Anglo-American academic establishment*, there was a centring of power in the loftiest ivory towers (notably Yale in the US) and a handful of sages. The most powerful of them was the Belgian immigrant (and Yale professor), Paul de Man.

7 Examples of how it works De Man published little. His first book, *Blindness and Insight*, appeared when he was in his early fifties. But his influence was radioactive in its penetration (and, some would argue, malignity). Famously de Man demonstrated the deconstructionist doctrine with an example from the TV show *All in the Family* (the American version of *Till Death Do Us Part*):

> 'When asked by his wife whether he wants to have his bowling shoes laced over or laced under*, Archie Bunker answers with a question: "What's the difference?" His wife replies by patiently explaining the difference between lacing over and lacing under, but provokes only ire*. "What's the difference?" did not ask for the difference but means instead "I don't give a damn* what the difference is."'

8 De Man then jumps, brilliantly, to the last lines of W. B. Yeats' poem, 'Among School Children':

> O body swayed to music, O brightening glance,
> How can we know the dancer from the dance?

Mrs Bunker might understand this as 'Please tell me the expert who can separate these two elements and come up with some names from the world of ballet.' The more knowledgeable reader might understand it as 'Dancer and dance are inseparable; they have merged into each other.' This second is not, of course, to be taken as the *authoritative* meaning of Yeats' poem. There can be no such thing – meaning is forever, as Derrida put it, 'deferred'. What de Man was illustrating by his Bunker–Yeats conjunction was the insoluble fragilities of meaning.

9 The intellectual excitements offered by deconstruction are clear. It put a wrecking ball* into the reader-critic's hand, particularly that of young academics, eager for some Oedipal intellectual mayhem*. There were those who viewed it as a benign 'Sturm und Drang*' interval – an exuberant clearing of the decks*; an 'everything must go!*' moment before the shop is stocked with entirely new wares.

10 In 1987, four years after de Man's death, deconstruction was hit by its own wrecking ball. A young Belgian scholar, Ortwin de Graef (initially a disciple*) turned up some 170 articles written by de Man during the Nazi occupation of Belgium – most of them for the country's leading newspaper, *Le Soir**. A handful of which looked suspiciously like party-line anti-Semitism*, notably a piece published on 4 March 1941, 'The Jews in Contemporary Literature',

75 which concluded:

> 'A solution to the Jewish problem that would lead to the creation of a Jewish colony isolated from Europe would not have, for the literary life of the West, regrettable consequences. It would lose, in all, some personalities of mediocre worth and would continue, as in the past, to
80 develop according to its higher laws of evolution.'

Even if he did not know the 'solution' his current employers had in mind, de Man, it was pointed out, could surely not but have noticed the current persecution of Belgian Jews, who had recently been required to mark themselves for execution by wearing the yellow star*.

85 **11** In the wake of de Graef's revelations, other skeletons were hauled out of the deceased de Man's cupboard*. Deconstruction was not destroyed by the revelation of de Man's wartime publications and other alleged malfeasance* (bigamy*, notably). But it was substantially deconstructed.

---

1 *'La Structure, le signe et le jeu dans le discours des sciences humaines'*：フランス語で
「人間諸科学の言説における構造、記号、戯れ」の意味。
International Colloquium on Critical Languages and the Sciences of Man：「批評言語・人間諸科学国際会議」
2 **theory**：「理論」 ▶解説
higher Froggy nonsense：「フランスらしい高尚ぶった戯言」 'Froggy'はフランス人の蔑称。
3 *doctrinaires*：「教義や理論を信じ込む人」
orthodoxy：「正統教義」
tenet：「（基礎となる）教理」
Zappism：ここでは本書の見出しで言及されるザップの独特な言い回しを指す。
inherently indeterminate：「内在的に決定不可能な」 ▶解説
4 **ad infinitum**：「無限に、永久に」
5 *écriture*：「書かれたもの」または「書くこと」を意味するフランス語。 ▶解説
the Flying Wallendas：「フライング・ワレンダス」20世紀前半から活動する綱渡りスタント集団。
6 **Anglo-American academic establishment**：「英米の学界」
7 **laced over or laced under**：「上結びか下結びか」靴紐を穴の上から通すか下から通すか。
ire：「怒り」
don't give a damn：「気にしない、どうでもいい」を意味するスラング。
9 **wrecking ball**：「（解体工事用の）鉄球」
Oedipal intellectual mayhem：「エディプス的な知的騒乱」 ▶解説

Strum und Drang：「疾風怒濤」18世紀後半のドイツの文学運動。▶解説
clearing of the decks：「甲板の片付け」闘争や活動の準備を含意する。
everything must go：売り尽くしセールの決まり文句。
❿ disciple：「弟子、信奉者」
Le Soir：「ル・ソワール紙」紙名はフランス語で「夕べ、夜」の意味。
anti-Semitism：「反ユダヤ主義」
the yellow star：ユダヤ人であることを示す「黄色い星」の着用が義務づけられたのは、実際には1942年以降。
⓫ other skeletons were hauled out of the deceased de Man's cupboard：'skeleton in the cupboard'（「秘密にすべきスキャンダル」）を踏まえた言い回し。
malfeasance：「悪事」
bigamy：「重婚」

Post-reading Vocabulary Check

> 日本語の意味に合う英文になるよう、次の中から適切な 動詞 を選び、必要に応じて形を変えなさい。

provoke ・ defer ・ merge ・ date ・ coalesce ・ quiver ・ go ・ plummet

1. 車は渓谷にまっすぐ落ちていった。
The car _____ into the canyon.

2. 決議は 11 月まで延期された。
The decision was _____ until November.

3. 彼女のふるまいは疑念を生じさせた。
Her behavior _____ suspicion.

4. 木の葉がそよ風に揺れていた。
The leaves were _____ in the breeze.

5. その運動はやがて一つの政党にまとまっていった。
The movement eventually _____ into a political party.

6. キリストの誕生日を特定するのは不可能である。
It is impossible to _____ the birth of Jesus.

7. 彼は朝のルーティンをこなした。
He _____ through his morning routine.

8. 空と海が一つに溶け合っていた。
The sky and the sea _____ into one.

> 下記の 形容詞または副詞 ＝英英・英日の語義が成立するように、空欄を埋めなさい。

1. i □□□□□□ ly = at first, originally「当初は」

2. a □□□□□ ary = random, haphazard「任意の、恣意的な」

3. analogous =s □□□□□□ , like「類似した」

4. l □□□□ = noble, very high「高尚な、そびえ立つ」

5. k □□□□□□□□ able = learned, well-read「物知りの、聡明な」

6. in □□□□□ able = inextricable, indivisible「分かちがたい、分離できない」

7. be □□□□ = mild, harmless「穏健な、無害の」

8. m □□□□□□□ = not very good「並みの、凡庸な」

9. a □□□□ ed = purported, presumed「（証拠は無いが）申し立てられている」

10. substantially = m □□□ ly, considerably「大体は、大幅に」

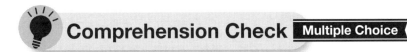

Comprehension Check [True or False]

下の英文が本文の内容として正しい場合はT、間違っている場合はFを選びましょう。

1. Jacques Derrida introduced deconstruction to America in 1966. (T / F)

2. Deconstruction first became popular in the non-academic world. (T / F)

3. Deconstruction explains that it is impossible not to fall into the abyss of unmeaningness. (T / F)

4. According to Paul de Man, certain readers can discover the authoritative meaning of Yeats' poem. (T / F)

5. Paul de Man's wartime publications were clearly anti-Semitic. (T / F)

Comprehension Check [Multiple Choice]

本文の内容に照らして最も正しいものを a 〜 c の中から選んで○をつけなさい。

1. Which of the following is true about 'theory'?
   a. Roland Barthes and Jacques Lacan demanded that their ideas be called 'theory'.
   b. 'Theory' was never influential in the US.
   c. The older American faculty were less enthusiastic about 'theory'.

2. Which is NOT true about the essential tenet of deconstruction?
   a. Any encounter with literature involves an endless process.
   b. Every literary text has meaning determined by its author.
   c. The meaning of a literary text is cancelled soon after it is constructed.

3. In the heyday of deconstruction,
   a. a handful of scholars in prestigious universities had power.
   b. deconstructionists ignored European philosophy.
   c. deconstruction was widely accepted outside the academic establishment in the US.

4. Archie Bunker was irritated by his wife because
   a. her explanation was incomprehensible.
   b. he did not want to have his bowling shoes laced at all.
   c. he did not care about the difference between laced over and laced under.

5. What 'deconstructed' deconstruction was

    a. young academics' intellectual revolt against more conventional scholars.

    b. the revelation of Paul de Man's Nazi membership.

    c. Paul de Man's politically suspicious articles and other private problems.

 ACTIVE LEARNING for Discussion

1. 第 7 パラグラフで引用されている Bunker 夫妻の会話について、Paul de Man はどのような ことの例としてこれを用いたのか、ペアまたはグループで話し合ってみましょう。

2. 第 3 パ ラ グ ラ フ 'every literary text is inherently indeterminate' や 第 8 パ ラ グ ラ フ 'meaning is forever ... "deferred"' について、自分のこれまでの読書体験や言語体験に照ら して、その考えに賛成できるかどうか、ペアまたはグループで話し合ってみましょう。

3. この章では宗教に関わる語彙が多く用いられています。そのことから、筆者の脱構築に対する 意見はどのようなものと考えられるか、ペアまたはグループで話し合ってみましょう。

 読むならまずこの一冊

ジャック・デリダ『グラマトロジーについて』足立和浩訳（現代思潮新社、上下巻）
広く誤解されてきたとされる脱構築。提唱者自身の言葉に触れてみよう。

CHAPTER **14**

新歴史主義

New Historicism

入植者ジョン・ロルフ (John Rolfe) がポカホンタス (Pocahontas) の父と交わした会話から、ニーチェ (Friedrich Vilhelm Nietzsche) の残した文書の中に見つかった「私は雨傘を忘れた」という走り書きまで、新歴史主義者たちは出来事や寓話をとらえて独自の仕方で再読し、微々たる細部の分析を通して、社会全体を統べる行動原則、論理や原動力までを明らかにする。H・アラム・ヴィーザー (H. Aram Veeser) によれば、これが新歴史主義の特徴である。それは 1970 年代に現れた批評の学派で、それ以降アカデミアの内外で、文学の議論において支配的な存在となった。

 Pre-reading Vocabulary Check

日本語の意味に合う英文になるよう、次の中から適切なものを選びなさい。必要に応じて形を変えなさい。

> glibly・epidemic・by-product・subversive・abolition・imperialism・
> unsettling・comprehensive

1. 不平等は資本主義によってやむを得ず生じた副産物だ。
Inequality is an inevitable ＿＿＿＿＿＿＿＿ of capitalism.

2. 疫病によって地域人口が減少した。
An ＿＿＿＿＿＿ led to depopulation of the area.

3. その組織は反体制分子とみなされていた。
The organization was considered a ＿＿＿＿＿＿ element.

4. その調査結果は、貿易に対する意見形成についての包括的な見方を提供する。
The survey result provides a ＿＿＿＿＿＿＿＿＿ view on trade attitude formation.

5. 帝国主義はヨーロッパの植民地支配の拡大を急速化させた。
＿＿＿＿＿＿＿＿ accelerated the European colonial expansion.

6. 死刑制度の廃止に消極的な国もある。
Some countries are reluctant about the ＿＿＿＿＿＿ of the death penalty.

7. テロのニュースは人心をかき乱した。
The news about a terrorist attack was very ＿＿＿＿＿＿ for people.

8. その政治家は流暢にしゃべるけれども、その内容はまるで意味不明だ。
The politician talks ＿＿＿＿＿＿ but what he says does not make sense at all.

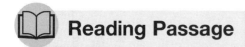

Reading Passage

🔊 Audio 2-06

1 Historicism versus new historicism   One's everyday reading is
conducted in a constant state of tension between the historical and the
ahistorical (critics, averse to using simple words when technical ones are to
hand, use the terms synchronic/diachronic* for this tension). What works
5 best? Should one create an imaginary time machine, twirl the lever, and
whisk back to the period in which the work of literature was created? Or
drag the work of literature into the clinic of the present, as something outside
time, place and historical accident?

2 Common sense instructs us that historicism is a fact of any reading. If you
10 find an old newspaper lining an antique chest of drawers, you look at the
headlines ('*Titanic** Sinks: Many Casualties') differently from this morning's
hot-off-the-press *Guardian** or *New York Times*. But why? They are all
newspapers.

3 Historicism has always been regarded as one of the handier tools in the
15 critic and reader's toolbox. Can one respond to *Moby-Dick* unless one knows
something of the early nineteenth-century whaling industry? The danger,
though, is that historicism explains things too glibly. If, for example, one
reads Jacobean tragedy* in terms of the gloom that descended on the country
after the death of Elizabeth (exacerbated by the rampant epidemic of 'pox', or
20 syphilis*), it closes the case too efficiently. Historicism won't explain the
crucial individual differences between the drama of John Webster, Thomas
Middleton and late Shakespeare.

4 New historicism's non-reductive approach   Historicism leads to
reductive readings – as if literature were merely a by-product. New
25 historicism is consciously un-reductive. It complicates rather than
simplifying. Primarily it does this by *reading* the historical circumstances of
literature as if they too were textual. A favoured slogan of the school is 'the
historicity of texts and the textuality* of history' (don't, incidentally, use it if
there's a bona fide* historian in earshot).

30 **5** How would a new historicist approach the plays – or, more accurately, the
'theatre' – of Elizabethan England? They might well begin by pointing out
where the Globe (Shakespeare's theatre) was situated – south of the river, in
Southwark*. In the seventeenth century this, on the city boundary, was also

where the taverns* and brothels* tended to be. What comes to mind is the red-light area in New Orleans* that gave birth to jazz. ₃₅

6 This 'liminality*' – urban edginess – explains the subversive nature of the drama of the period, new historicists suggest. Parliament, the Inns of Court, Westminster Cathedral* were across the water. Visible, but within the pale*. The theatres were neither in, nor out, but on the fence. In short, the new historicist would say, a ride on the 68 bus across Waterloo Bridge* (our new ₄₀ historicist could make much of that imperialist structure*, as well) will be as useful as a whole page of notes in the Arden edition of Shakespeare*.

7 A Shakespearian illustration   When Hamlet instructs Ophelia to 'get thee to a nunnery, go' (punning on the nunnery/brothel street slang*), his brutality gains resonance from the fact that there were brothels next door. ₄₅ One particularly famous house of ill repute* – doing good business during Shakespeare's day – was the Cardinal's Cap and the Bell* (it was allegedly patronized by the star actor Edward Alleyn – who was also a brothel owner).

8 All this risky business – together with the wildest taverns and a lot of crime – happened south of the river (the 'wrong side of the tracks'* in post- ₅₀ railway slang). What distinguishes new historicism from old historicism is its interest in the (actively) subversive rather than the (passively) reflective aspects of culture. Like taverns and brothels, Elizabethan/Jacobean drama is inherently dissident and anti-authoritarian. Hence the strict censorship under which the British playwright worked until, incredibly, the abolition of ₅₅ the Lord Chamberlain's Office* in 1969.

9 The critic who founded new historicism, Stephen Greenblatt, recalls being inspired to do so while teaching a course on Marxist* aesthetics. One detects a sophisticated version of the familiar base/superstructure model*. One of the more influential new historicist interpretations (associated with ₆₀ Greenblatt) is to read *The Tempest* as a subversive critique of imperialism – a twist that, perversely, ennobles Caliban (something routinely reflected in contemporary productions of the play), aligning Shakespeare with Frantz Fanon (advocate of radical *négritude*). In a 1974 National Theatre* (London) performance, Caliban was made up, Janus* style, with one side of his face a ₆₅ version of Rousseau's noble savage, the other side a repulsive ape. The effect was unsettling.

10 Neo-Marxism* (often watered down) is one distinguishing mark. The other salient feature distinguishing new historicism from traditional historical

70 approaches is its characteristic focus on small, in themselves, incidental elements in the literary design. The old historicists massed as much contextual data as they could. For the new historicists, a single datum can have as much, or more, illustrative value as a mountain of data.

11 The guiding light here is not Marx, but the anthropologist Clifford Geertz,
75 and his essay on a cockfight, from which he deduces large interpretations about Balinese culture. In literature there are also apparently incidental aspects that are illustrative.

12 The objection lodged against new historicism (particularly by historians) is that it is lazy, unsystematic history.

80 **13** Its approach to the past is that of the magpie to nest-building* – a piece here, a piece there, nothing comprehensive. The objections from cultural conservatives target its leftist liberalism (or worse). It is the literary criticism of the revolution. New historicism remains, however, one of the most accessible and illuminating of recent critical innovations.

---

1 synchronic/diachronic：「共時的／通時的」▶解説
2 *Titanic*：「タイタニック号」1912 年に北大西洋で沈没した豪華客船。世紀最大の海難事故としてしばしば映画化されてきた。▶ Chapter 1 Mimesis
2 *Guardian*：「ガーディアン」イギリスの大手新聞。
3 Jacobean tragedy：「ジャコビアン時代の悲劇」▶解説
'pox', or syphilis：「梅毒」pox は痘一般も指すが、ジャコビアン期に特に流行したのは梅毒とされ、当時の演劇作品でもしばしば言及された。
4 textuality：「テクスト性」▶解説
bona fide：「本物の」
5 Southwark：「サザーク」ロンドン中部のテムズ川南岸に面する、かつてグローブ座が位置したエリアを指す。
tavern：「庶民的な居酒屋」
brothel：「売春宿」
the red-light area in New Orleans：「ニューオーリンズの赤線地帯」1897 年から 1917 年まで売春地区だったストーリーヴィルを指す。州外からの来訪者が数多く訪れて初めてジャズを聴いたことから、ジャズの誕生地とみなされることがある。
6 liminality：「リミナリティ」▶解説
Parliament, the Inns of Court, Westminster Cathedral：「国会、法学院、ウェストミンスター寺院」政治的、法的、宗教的規範を代表するような場所を列記している。
within the pale：「法の枠内、埒内」
the 68 bus across Waterloo Bridge：「ウォータールー橋を渡る 68 番のバス」ロンドン市バス 68 番の路線はイートン方面行きで、ウォータールー橋を経由している。
that imperialist structure：「あの帝国主義的構造」ウォータールー橋の名が、イギリスを含む連合軍がナポレオン率いるフランス軍を破ったワーテルローの戦いの、帝国主義的列強の覇権争いとしての側面に言及していると思われる。

the Arden edition of Shakespeare：「アーデン版シェイクスピア」シェイクスピアの作品集の中でも豊富な注釈が付いた学術性の高い版。

❼ The nunnery/brothel street slang：「尼寺を売春宿の隠語とする街場の言い回し」

house of ill repute：「売春宿」

the Cardinal's Cap and the Bell：グローブ座付近にあったとされる売春宿。

❽ the 'wrong side of the tracks'：「町の貧しい地区」列車が登場してからは、「線路の向こう側の発展していない地区」という意味でこの言い回しが使われ出した。

the Lord Chamberlain's Office：「チャンバーレイン卿執務室」1969年に演劇検閲法が廃止されるまで、イギリスで上演されるすべての演劇の検閲を行っていた王室内の部署。

❾ Maxist：「マルクス主義の」▶ Chapter 7 Base/Superstructure ▶解説 Base/superstructure

base/superstructure model ▶ Chapter 7 Base/Superstructure

National Theatre：「ナショナル・シアター」ロンドン、サウスバンクにある国立劇場。数々のシェイクスピア作品の名高いヴァージョンを上演。

Janus：「ヤヌス」ローマ神話に登場する、頭の前後に顔を持つ神。

❿ Neo Marxisim：(New Marxism とも)「新マルクス主義」▶ Chapter 7 Base/Superstructure

⓭ the magpie to nest-building：「カササギの巣作りのようなアプローチ」「カササギの巣」はイギリスのおとぎ話の一つで、賢いカササギに鳥たちが巣の作り方を聞きに来たが、一部分終えるたびに一羽ずつ去ってしまい、全体の作り方を誰もちゃんと学ばなかったというもの。本文では、過去や歴史への包括的なアプローチを持たない新歴史主義を揶揄するために使われている。

Post-reading Vocabulary Check

➤ 日本語の意味に合う英文になるよう、次の中から適切な 動詞 を選び、必要に応じて形を変えなさい。

conduct・exacerbate・situate・patronize・distinguish・inspire・align・target

1. 研究を行なうのに十分な環境があります。
I have sufficient environment for _____ my research.

2. そのテレビ番組は明らかに中年視聴者層を対象にしている。
The TV show apparently _____ the middle-age audience.

3. 彼女は若い芸術家たちに特段の支援を与えた。
She _____ young artists in particular.

4. 彼のケンカ腰の態度は状況を悪化させただけだった。
His confrontational attitude only _____ the situation.

5. 文書の基本的なレイアウトは、各文を左寄せにすることです。
The standard layout of a document is the text being _____ to the left.

6. そのバンドの新しいアルバムはカントリーに影響されていた。
The band's new album was _____ by country music.

7. 彼女と双子の姉妹の見分けがつかなかった。
I could not _____ her from her twin sister.

8. この研究は同時代の女性作家たちをフェミニズムの文脈に位置付けることを目指す。
This study seeks to _____ the contemporary female writers in the feminist context.

➤ 下記の 名詞、形容詞または副詞 ＝英英・英日の語義が成立するように、空欄を埋めなさい。

1. a □□□□□ = opposed, reluctant「きらって、避けて」

2. g □□□□ = despondency, dimness「陰気さ、暗さ」

3. r □□□□□□ = uncontrolled, violent「激しい、猛威を振るう」

4. r □□□□□□□□ = importance, profundity「重要性、意義深さ」

5. a □□□□□□□□ =reportedly, supposedly「伝えられるところでは」

6. d □□□□□□□□ = disagreeing, objecting「反対する、反体制の」

7. s □□□□□□ = notable, important「顕著な、重要な」

8. i □□□□□□□□□□ = subsidiary「二次的な、偶発的な」

Comprehension Check **True or False**

下の英文が本文の内容として正しい場合は T、間違っている場合は F を選びましょう。

1. The problem of historicism is that it explains history in an overtly-complicated way. (T / F)

2. New historicism concentrates on minute details of history. (T / F)

3. New historicism tends to think cultural texts simply reflect the time period in which they were produced. (T / F)

4. Caliban is often vilified in new historicist interpretations. (T / F)

5. New historicism has been criticized for its superficial approach toward history. (T / F)

Comprehension Check **Multiple Choice**

本文の内容に照らして最も正しいものを a ～ c の中から選んで○をつけなさい。

1. According to the idea of textuality, which one of the following is the best subject of a new historicist reading?
   a. a literary work
   b. the south bank of London
   c. Both **a** and **b**

2. Which of the following is not located near the Globe?
   a. taverns
   b. brothels
   c. Parliament

3. According to the author, what new historicism tends to take interest in in a culture is
   a. its rebellious aspect.
   b. its submissive aspect.
   c. its commemorative aspect.

4. Which of the following authors is often associated with new historicism?
   a. John Webster
   b. Thomas Middleton
   c. William Shakespeare

5. Clifford Geertz's field work is comparable to the new historicist approach because

   a. it celebrates the values of marginalized non-Western cultures.

   b. it utilizes seemingly unimportant details to draw larger interpretations.

   c. it is lacking in a systematic historical analysis.

 ACTIVE LEARNING for Discussion

1. 本文中で挙げられていた歴史主義と新歴史主義の違いをペアまたはグループで話し合い、改めて整理してみましょう。何が改善されたのでしょうか。また、ふたつの間で変わっていない点はありますか。

2. 新歴史主義が明らかにしたように、あらゆるものを「テクスト」として読解できるとすれば、どんなものを読んでみたいですか。ペアまたはグループで話し合ってみましょう。

3. 本文ではイギリス文学の例が紹介されていましたが、日本文学を新歴史主義のアプローチで読むとすれば、具体的にどんな作品がいいと思いますか。ペアまたはグループで話し合ってみましょう。

 読むならまずこの一冊

ウィリアム・シェイクスピア『テンペスト』小田島雄志訳（白水 U ブックス）
本章の Reading Passage を参照しつつ、新歴史主義的アプローチで行くと各登場人物が何を象徴しうるのか、またそれとはまったく異なる読み方をするとすればどうなるか、考えてみよう。

CHAPTER 15

性の政治学

Sexual Politics

Kate Millett At Demonstration © Fred W. McDarrah
View of American feminist activist, author, and artist Kate
Millett (1934 - 2017) as she attends an equal rights
demonstration, New York, New York, June 27, 1971. She
holds a sign that reads 'Hi Mom, Join Us.' (Photo by Fred
W. McDarrah/Getty Images)

大学は修道院の機関として始まった。中世の女子修道院には学識も筆写室も啓蒙家も図書館も存在せず、読み書きのできる人もほとんどいなかった。イギリスとアメリカの高等教育（大学）に女性が入ってきたのは、まずは英文科であった。（例えば、理論物理学とは違って）英文学は、伝統的に「重要ではない」教科として見下されていたという事実にもかかわらず、1960 年代までには、1966 年に（『女性らしさの神話』[The Feminine Mystique] の著者であるベティ・フリーダン [Betty Friedan] の指揮のもと）設立された NOW [全米女性組織] のような構想に熱狂的に反応した若い研究者たちの間ではかなりの存在感を誇っていた。

 Pre-reading Vocabulary Check

日本語の意味に合う英文になるよう、次の中から適切なものを選びなさい。必要に応じて形を変えなさい。

---

decade · liberation · assert · persecution · allude ·
obscenity · survey · execution

---

1. 彼女は自分の無罪を強く主張した。
She _____ her innocence of the crime.

2. ヘンリー・ミラーの回想録はわいせつを理由に発禁になった。
Henry Miller's memoir was banned for _____ .

3. ここ 10 年間で IT は大きな発展を遂げた。
There has been much IT development during the last _____ .

4. 彼のスピーチはシェイクスピアに間接的に言及していた。
His speech _____ to Shakespeare.

5. 日本における死刑執行の方法は絞首刑である。
The means of _____ in Japan is hanging.

6. 背景をざっと概観しましょう。
Let's make a _____ of the background.

7. シモーヌ・ド・ボーヴォワールは女性解放運動の草分けの一人である。
Simone de Beauvoir is one of the pioneers of the women's _____ movement.

8. ニューヨーク市にはナチスの迫害を逃れてきた亡命者がたくさんいた。
There were many refugees from Nazi _____ in New York City.

Reading Passage

🔊 Audio 2-07

1 The angry origins It was no accident that feminism arrived on the scene when it did. The 1960s was a decade of 'political liberation', with the Civil Rights Act of 1964, and political protest (principally against the Vietnam War).

5 **2** The term 'sexual politics' was the title of a book published by Kate Millett in 1970. It began as a doctoral thesis at Columbia University in New York. Millett was a student during the 'Years of the Young Rebels'*.

3 She took her data from across the canon* of literary studies – all of her principal examples being male. Millett opened her monograph with
10 'instances'. The first instance was from Henry Miller's 'raunchy' memoir *Sexus*. This was a work that had been banned in the US until the 'liberalizing' *Lady Chatterley* court cases of 1959–60*, which made 'raunch' legal.

4 The passage Millett chose to open her case describes Miller lying in his
15 bath, summoning his paramour*, and brutally screwing* her:

> 'I left the stockings on – it made her more lascivious* looking, the Cranach type. I lay back and pulled her on top of me. She was just like a bitch in heat* … as I pulled away I left the mark of my teeth on her beautiful white ass. Not a word spoken.'

20 **5** What, precisely, had been 'liberated'? enquired Millett. She went on to answer with a single word: 'patriarchy*' – a system of female oppression stretching as far back as literary (and Biblical) texts could take us. The issue was not obscenity, but 'politics' – who was in charge in the scene above?

6 Sexual relationships were not, as Millett saw it, biological, but rooted in
25 'power' – or, as she preferred to call it, 'force*' (a word with closer relation to 'rape'). 'The history of patriarchy,' she grimly asserted, 'presents a variety of cruelties and barbarities: the suttee* execution in India, the crippling deformity of foot-binding* in China, the lifelong ignominy of the veil in Islam, or the widespread persecution of sequestration, the gynaeceum, and
30 purdah*.' Literature (predominantly written by men) was patriarchy's mirror, its apology, and an argument for* its continuation.

7 Sexual politics and British literary criticism In the UK, at the same period, a young English lecturer at Warwick University (an institution, like Columbia, that the newspapers liked to label a 'hotbed') published *The*
35 *Female Eunuch*. Germaine Greer's doctorate had been on Shakespeare's comedy. *A Midsummer Night's Dream* was a play of particular interest to

her. Traditionally 'the Dream' had been regarded as the most charmingly harmless of Shakespeare's fantasies. Greer read it differently. The action opens with the impending marriage of Theseus (ruler of Athens) and Hippolyta – formerly Queen of the Amazons*. She has been abducted*, 40 literally* 'raped'. The preparations are interrupted by the case of a girl who refuses to marry the man her father has chosen for her. She is casually condemned to* death. Among the fairies, Oberon is angry with his wife Titania. He dopes* her, and laughs as she submits to be (publicly) ravished* by a donkey – traditionally seen as a beast with a monstrous penis. 45

8 The English school*, represented by Greer, tended to see their ancestress as Virginia Woolf: a commentator who was commonsensical rather than ideological. In America it was Friedan (and behind her, Simone de Beauvoir).

9 Anger such as Millett's was the kindling*. A more programmatic polemic* was framed by Elaine Showalter. Showalter recalled, as an undergraduate, 50 being instructed by a male lecturer that Woolf's *Mrs Dalloway* was the study of an inadequate wife. As a professor of English at Princeton, Showalter edited the novel. She discerned – from hints carefully embedded in the narrative – that it was the study of a woman going through menopause*.

10 Keep out, men?   Women, it was implied, had a privileged access to texts 55 written by women. Showalter elevated this insight into a panoramic survey of women novelists, *A Literature of Their Own* ('our own', that is). Presses in Britain and America (notably the women-run collective*, Virago) set out to* 'recover' this literature, bringing it back into print and thus more readily into the curriculum. Literary feminism ('gynocriticism*'), argued Showalter, 60 progressed through three phases: feminine/feminist/female*.

11 A similarly wide-ranging conspectus* was attempted by Sandra Gilbert and Susan Gubar in their manifesto work, *The Madwoman in the Attic*. Their title alludes to the first Mrs Rochester ('Bertha Mason'), in *Jane Eyre*. As conventionally perceived, in the century after the novel's publication, she was 65 a figure of Gothic horror*, a monster.

12 Read with modern subtlety (aided by post-Freudian insight*), Bertha took on two new characters. She was the oppressed woman of history who – when she rebelled – was thought merely mad. Secondly she was the raging protest within Jane that, all her life, Jane had been 'manfully' suppressing. Jane was 70 the eunuch, Bertha the woman *furiosa**. Bertha Mason in her attic (odd that she is rarely called 'Bertha Rochester') was a prime example, but read carefully, all great literature – from Chaucer to Anna Karenina – demanded new reading and reinterpretation along these lines. That, in turn, required academic/critical power. It happened as women assumed equal professorial 75 status. Showalter, to take one example, became head of the department at Princeton, where her colleagues were Toni Morrison and Joyce Carol Oates. In 2010, over half the literary editors in the dozen or so opinion-forming review pages in the UK national press were women (50 years earlier, the figure was precisely zero). In the publishing world women assumed for the first time CEO* roles in multinational companies. They might still, as Spivak puts it*, feel themselves somewhat 'outside' but they were, undeniably, in the literary machine*, at last. Even running it.

❷ the 'Years of the Young Rebels'：「若き叛逆者たちの年」 ▶解説
❸ canon：「キャノン」 ▶ Chapter 8 The Canon
Lady Chatterley court cases of 1959–60：「1959–60 年の『チャタレイ夫人』裁判事件」
❹ paramour：「愛人」
screw：「セックスする」
lascivious：「扇情的な」
bitch in heat：「発情期の雌犬」
❺ patriarchy：「家父長制度」
❻ force：「力（強制力）」cf. power
suttee：「サティー」 ▶解説
crippling deformity of foot-binding：「足を縛って不自由に変形させること」纏足。
sequestration, the gynaeceum, and purdah：「（古代ギリシアの）婦人部屋や（インドの）パルダといった社会隔離の習慣」
argument for...：「…に賛成する意見」
❼ the Amazons：「アマゾン」ギリシア神話に出てくる女性だけの部族。
abduct：「誘拐する」
literally：「（誇張して）事実上、文字通り」
condemn...to~：「…に~の判決を下す」
dope：「薬を盛る」この場合、惚れ薬をかける。
ravish：「夢中にさせる」
❽ school：「学派」
❾ kindling：「発火点」
polemic：「論争」
menopause：「更年期」
❿ collective：「（労働者が運営する）共同体企業」
set out to...：「…しようと試みる」
gynocriticism：「ガイノクリティシズム」 ▶解説
three phases: feminine/feminist/female：「3段階、すなわち女性的段階／フェミニズムの段階／女の段階」 ▶解説
⓫ conspectus：「概観」
Gothic horror：「ゴシック・ホラー」 ▶ Chapter 5 Gothic
⓬ post-Freudian insight：「フロイト以後の精神分析的洞察」 ▶解説
furiosa：「怒り狂った」スペイン語の女性形の形容詞（英）furious
CEO：「最高経営責任者（chief executive officer）」
as one puts it：「人が言うように」
the literary machine：「（大学（院）の）文学組織の中枢」 ▶解説

Post-reading Vocabulary Check

➤ 日本語の意味に合う英文になるよう、次の中から適切な 動詞 を選び、必要に応じて形を変えなさい。

| summon・enquire・oppress・discern・assume・embed・ban・imply |

1. 彼は校長室に呼ばれた。

He was _____ to the principal's office.

2. 聖書に埋め込まれた深い意味に彼女は気づいた。

She found out the deeper meaning _____ in the Scripture.

3. 政府は公共の場での喫煙を禁止した。

The government _____ smoking in all public places.

4. その２つの意見の間に違いを認めることができない。

I can _____ no difference between the two opinions.

5. プアホワイトは肌の色ではなく彼らの属する階級ゆえに虐げられている。

Poor whites are _____ not because of their skin color but because of their class position.

6. 彼女はその商品の値段を訊いた。

She _____ the price of the item.

7. 彼は大統領に就任した。

He _____ the presidency.

8. ほのめかすというのは、間接的に何かを示唆することを意味する。

To _____ means to suggest something indirectly.

➤ 下記の 形容詞または副詞 ＝英英・英日の語義が成立するように、空欄を埋めなさい。

1. r □□□□□ = obscene「わいせつな」

2. bi □□□□□□□ = inherent「生物学上の」

3. predominantly = m □□□ ly, mostly「主に、大部分は」

4. i □□□□□ ing = upcoming , approaching「差し迫っている」

5. in □□□□□□□□ = insufficient, lacking「不十分な、不出来な」

6. pri □□□□□□□ = qualified, authorized「特権的な」

7. notably = e □□□□□□ lly, particularly「とりわけ」

8. c □□□□□□□□□□ lly = traditionally, commonly「慣習的に」

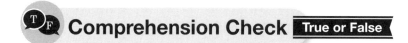

Comprehension Check True or False

下の英文が本文の内容として正しい場合は T、間違っている場合は F を選びましょう。

1. The anti-Vietnam War movement had an influence on the rise of feminism in the US. (T / F)

2. Foot-binding in China is a product of patriarchy. (T / F)

3. Literature made a contribution to the prevalence of patriarchy. (T / F)

4. *A Midsummer Night's Dream* is full of sexual assaults against men. (T / F)

5. The rise of literary feminism happened outside universities. (T / F)

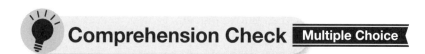

Comprehension Check Multiple Choice

本文の内容に照らして最も正しいものを a 〜 c の中から選んで○をつけなさい。

1. Which of the following does NOT apply to Millett's opinions?

   a. Men should be in charge of romantic relationship.

   b. Women have been oppressed in patriarchy.

   c. Sexual politics is the issue of *Sexus*.

2. *A Midsummer Night's Dream* is less likely to be seen as a charmingly harmless comedy

   a. in a male dominated society.

   b. in a society with diversity.

   c. in a patriarchal society.

3. Which is NOT true about Elaine Showalter?

   a. She thought that women have a better understanding of texts written by women.

   b. Her professorship at Princeton gave her a voice.

   c. She offered a new interpretation of Bertha Mason in *Jane Eyre*.

4. Conventionally, Bertha Mason was regarded as

   a. a monster.

   b. a heroine in Gothic horror.

   c. a victim.

5. Which of the following was less likely to happen when women assumed a professorship in the English Departments?

   a. teaching more literary works by female writers in a classroom

   b. re-reading great literature

   c. abandoning all patriarchal customs that had oppressed women

 ## ACTIVE LEARNING for Discussion

1. 第6パラグラフ 'Literature (predominantly written by men) was patriarchy's mirror, its apology, and an argument for its continuation.' を踏まえて、大学によって「誰が」「どのような文学作品」を教えるかによって、どのような違いが生まれるのか、ペアまたはグループで話し合ってみましょう。

2. 第12パラグラフ 'Jane was the eunuch, Bertha the woman *furiosa*.' について、なぜ Jane は「去勢された男（eunuch）」とされ、一方で Bertha は「怒り狂った（furiosa）」という女性形で形容されているのか、その意図するところや効果をペアまたはグループで話し合ってみましょう。

3. ここでは 'sexual politics' における権力構造が、主に「男性／女性」という二項対立で論じられています。身近な例や知っている作品を通して、この構図をより広く多様な権力構造に発展させることができるか、ペアまたはグループで話し合ってみましょう。

 ## 読むならまずこの一冊

シャーロット・ブロンテ『ジェーン・エア』（岩波文庫、光文社古典新訳文庫、新潮文庫など）
〈Bertha Mason〉はモンスターなのか？　迫害された女性性の象徴なのか？

APPENDIX

❖ Reading Passage に登場する人名・作品名・用語には下線を引いています❖

Chapter 1: Mimesis

作家・(登場) 人物・作品リスト

Aristotle：「アリストテレス (384–322BC)」ギリシアの哲学者。プラトン門下生。政治学から天文学まで多岐にわたる学問の基礎を築き、「万学の祖」と呼ばれる。『詩学』(*The Poetics*) は悲劇などを考察した著作。

The Odyssey：「『オデュッセイア』」ホメロス (Homer) の作とされる紀元前8世紀ごろに成立した叙事詩。

Plato：「プラトン (428/427–348/347BC)」ギリシアの哲学者。ソクラテス (Socrates, 470頃–399BC) の弟子であり師の思想を対話篇として残した。人間が感受する事物は真の実在ではないとするイデア論を形成し、哲学者の統治する理想国家を説いた。『国家』(*The Republic*) はプラトン中期の対話篇。ほかに『ソクラテスの弁明』(*Apology of Socrates*)、『饗宴』(*The Symposium*) など。

Mark Edmundson：「マーク・エドマンドソン (1952–)」米国の英米文学者。

[Lev Nikolayevich] Tolstoy：「レフ・ニコラエヴィチ・トルストイ (1828–1910)」帝政ロシアの作家。あらゆる社会階層の人々が登場する激動の歴史を壮大に描いた大河小説『戦争と平和』(*War and Peace*, 1865–69) や人妻アンナの不倫の恋を中心に、人間はいかに生きるべきかなどの壮大なテーマを扱った『アンナ・カレーニナ』(*Anna Karenina*, 1875–77) などがある。

Graham Greene：「グレアム・グリーン (1904–91)」英国のカトリック小説家・劇作家。『第三の男』(*The Third Man*, 1949)、『情事の終わり』(*The End of the Affair*, 1951) など。

Leonardo DiCaprio：「レオナルド・ディカプリオ (1974–)」米国の俳優。ジェイムズ・キャメロン (James Francis Cameron, 1954–) 監督・脚本による『タイタニック』(*Titanic*, 1997) では英国女優ケイト・ウィンスレット (Kate Winslet, 1975–) とともに主演を務めた。

[John] Milton：「ジョン・ミルトン (John Milton, 1608–74)」代表作に叙事詩『失楽園』(*Paradise Lost*, 1667, 1674)。劇詩『闘技士サムソン』(*Samson Agonistes*, 1671) は旧約聖書『士師記』中の盲目のサムソンの死を主題に、コロスや「三一致の規則」の採用などギリシア悲劇の形式で著されている。

Pride and Prejudice：「『高慢と偏見』(1813)」英国の作家ジェーン・オースティン (Jane Austen, 1775-1817) の小説。ベネット家五人姉妹の次女エリザベスと名門の資産家ダーシーが互いに対して抱く偏見や高慢を克服して結ばれるさまを描く作家の代表作。

George Orwell：「ジョージ・オーウェル (1903–50)」本名 Eric Arthur Blair。英国の作家・エッセイスト。スターリン専制政治を風刺した『動物農場』(*Animal Farm*, 1945) や近未来のディストピアを描いた『1984』(*1984*, 1949) など。「鯨の腹のなかで」('Inside the Whale', 1940) などのエッセイも評価が高い。

Leviathan：「リヴァイアサン」旧約聖書『ヨブ記』などに現れる海棲の怪物。

[Aleksandr Isayevich] Solzhenitsyn：「アレクサンドル・イサーエヴィチ・ソルジェニーツィン（1918-2008）」ソ連・ロシアの小説家。ノーベル賞受賞（1970）、『収容所列島』（1973-75）などでソ連批判を行なった。

James Joyce：「ジェイムズ・ジョイス（1882-1941）」アイルランドの作家。『ユリシーズ』（*Ulysses*, 1922）は「意識の流れ」の手法を用い、モダニズム文学に多大な影響を与えた。他に『若き芸術家の肖像』（*A Portrait of the Artist as a Young Man*, 1916）、『フィネガンズ・ウェイク』（*Finnegans Wake*, 1939）など。

Bertolt Brecht：「ベルトルト・ブレヒト（1898-1956）」ドイツの劇作家・詩人。作曲家クルト・ヴァイル（Kurt Weill, 1900-50）との共作『三文オペラ』（*Die Dreigroschenoper*, 1928）など。「異化効果」の提唱者として知られる。

解説

category error：「カテゴリー錯誤」ある属性を、その属性を有せないものに帰するという意味論的・存在論的錯誤。

the philosopher-king：「哲人王」プラトンが提唱した「正義」を実現するための哲人の王。

the status of what another novelist, in her opening sentence, called 'a truth universally acknowledged'：オースティン『高慢と偏見』冒頭第1行（It is a truth universally acknowledged, that a single man in possession of a good fortune, must be in want of a wife.）を踏まえている。

'the heart of the matter'：グリーンの恋愛小説『事件の核心』（*The Heart of the Matter*, 1948）のもじり。

Mills and Boon：「ミルズ＆ブーン」ロマンス小説で有名な英国の出版社。

the Soviet 'Writers' Union'：「ソヴィエト連邦作家同盟（Soviet Union of Writers）」は1934年結成。社会的リアリズムを旨とし諸分野の作家が加盟。1991年ソ連崩壊とともに解散。

modernist：モダニストはモダニズムの信奉者・実践者。英米文学におけるモダニズムは1910年代から第一次世界大戦を経て1930年代にかけて、大胆な性の表現を含むさまざまなテーマを「意識の流れ」等の新手法を取り入れながら、実験的・野心的に扱った文学運動。

'silence, *exile*, and cunning'：『若き芸術家の肖像』中、主人公スティーヴン・ディーダラスが芸術観を述べる箇所からの引用。

Chapter 2: Ambiguity

作家・（登場）人物・作品リスト

Uncle Tom's Cabin：「『アンクル・トムの小屋』（1852）」ハリエット・ビーチャー・ストウ（Harriet Beecher Stowe, 1811–96）の小説。黒人奴隷アンクル・トム（Uncle Tom）の半生を描いた作品で、奴隷制の悲惨さを伝え、南北戦争前夜のアメリカで奴隷解放へと世論を傾け、リンカーン大統領から「南北戦争を引き起こした女性」と評されたという逸話が残っている。しかしながら、白人に従順なトムのキャラクターは公民権運動あたりから批判の対象にもなっている。

Jack Kerouac：「ジャック・ケルアック（1922–69）」ビート・ジェネレーションを代表する米国の小説家・詩人。アメリカを気ままに放浪する半ば自伝的な青春小説『路上』（*On the Road*, 1957）が代表作。

T. S. Eliot：「T・S・エリオット（1888–1965）」米国出身の英国の詩人・文芸批評家。長編詩『荒地』（*The Waste Land*, 1922）が代表作。

[William] Shakespeare：「ウィリアム・シェイクスピア（1564–1616）」英国の劇作家・詩人であり、『ハムレット』（*Hamlet*）を含む四大悲劇をはじめ、『真夏の夜の夢』（*A Midsummer Night's Dream*）や『ロミオとジュリエット』（*Romeo and Juliet*）など有名な戯曲が多数。『ハムレット』は主人公ハムレット（Hamlet）の父を殺し、母を奪って王位についた叔父クローディアス（Claudius）に復讐を遂げるというのがプロットである。

Oscar Wilde：「オスカー・ワイルド（1854–1900）」アイルランド生まれ。19世紀末英国文学の代表的な作家・劇作家・詩人。代表作に『サロメ』「幸福な王子」など。

[Samuel Taylor] Coleridge：「サミュエル・テイラー・コールリッジ（1772–1834）」英国ロマン派の詩人・批評家。

William Empson：「ウィリアム・エンプソン（1906–84）」英国の批評家、詩人。代表作に『曖昧の七つの型』（*Seven Types of Ambiguity*, 1930）。

Gerard Manley Hopkins：「ジェラード・マンリ・ホプキンス（1844–89）」英国ヴィクトリア朝の詩人。「チョウゲンボウ」（'The Windhover', 1877）の作者。

[Sigmund] Freud：「ジークムント・フロイト（1856–1939）」オーストリアの神経学者で、精神分析学の創始者。人間の心理の中で特に無意識の領域に注目した。

Nero：「ネロ（37–68）」第5代ローマ皇帝。初めは善政を行なったが、次第に残虐と淫蕩の限りを尽くし、母小アグリッピナ（Agrippina）と妃を殺害し、キリスト教徒を迫害した暴君。

Terry Eagleton：「テリー・イーグルトン（1943–　）」英国の文芸批評家。構造主義、記号論などフランス現代思想の影響を受けながら、マルクス主義の立場で評論を行なう。著作に『文学とは何か』（*Literary Theory: An Introduction*, 1983）など。

[John] Donne：「ジョン・ダン（1572–1631）」機知や唐突な比喩が特徴的な形而上詩人の代表格であり、形而上詩人には他にジョージ・ハーバート（George Herbert, 1593–1633）やアンドルー・マーヴェル（Andrew Marvell, 1621–78）がいる。

解説

Beat Generation：「ビート・ジェネレーション（ビート世代）」とは、1950年代、それまでの因習的な価値観に反発し、気ままな放浪生活を送った若者たちのこと。本文に出てくるジャック・ケルアックやアレン・ギンズバーグ（Allen Ginsberg, 1926-97）などの作家・詩人たちのグループを指す言葉でもある。

Oedipus complex：「エディプス・コンプレックス」とは、フロイトが提示した概念で、幼年期の子供（特に男児とされることが多い）が、母親に対する思慕の情から、父親に対して強く対抗心を抱く傾向を指す。元々は、ギリシア悲劇の『オイディプス王』（Oedipus Rex）がそうとは知らずに王である父を殺し、自身の母と結婚した近親相姦的なエピソードに由来する。

thou：thou は古語で you（第二人称単数主格）。thou（主格）、thy（l. 59）（所有格）、thee（目的格）。

practical criticism：「実践批評」米国では新批評あるいはニュー・クリティシズム（New Criticism）とも呼ばれ、作家の伝記的事実や、社会や政治的なコンテクストから作品を切り離して、作品世界に即して批評する方法。

close reading：「精読」テクストの短い一節を詳細に読み込み解釈することを指す。

Augustan age：「オーガスタン時代」とは、ウェルギリウス（Virgil, 70-19BC ▶ Chapter 4 Epic）やホラティウス（Quintus Horatius Flaccus, 65-8BC）など多くの詩人・哲学者を生んだローマ帝国初代皇帝アウグストゥス（Augustus, 63BC-14, 在位27BC-14）の時代を元々意味し、そこから一国の文芸隆盛時代（特に古代ギリシャ・ローマの芸術を規範とする古典主義の文学が隆盛した時代）を指す。英国では18世紀前半の古典主義隆盛の時代をそのように呼ぶことがある。アレクサンダー・ポープ（Alexander Pope, 1688-1744 ▶ Chapter 4 Epic, Chapter 11 Metafiction）や、小説『ガリヴァー旅行記』（Gulliver's Travels, 1726）で有名なジョナサン・スウィフト（Jonathan Swift, 1667-1745）、サミュエル・ジョンソン（Samuel Johnson, 1709-84 ▶ Chapter 8 The Canon）などが代表格。

Chapter 3: Narrative / Story

作家・（登場）人物・作品リスト

[Samuel] Richardson：「サミュエル・リチャードソン（1689-1761）」英国の作家。近代小説勃興期の代表的文学者のひとり。登場人物が互いに送り合った手紙によって作品を構成する書簡体小説（epistolary novel）の代表作『パミラ』（*Pamela*, 1740）、『クラリッサ』（*Clarissa*, 1748）の作者として知られる。

[Henry] Fielding：「ヘンリー・フィールディング（1707-54）」英国の作家。リチャードソンと並び、近代小説勃興期の代表的文学者のひとり。リチャードソンの『パミラ』をパロディ化した『シャミラ』（*Shamela*, 1741）のほか、代表作『トム・ジョーンズ』（*The History of Tom Jones, a Foundling*, 1749）などが有名。

Bleak House：「『荒涼館』（1852-53）」ヴィクトリア朝の初期から中期を代表する英国の作家チャールズ・ディケンズ（Charles Dickens, 1812-70）の小説。ディケンズには『オリヴァー・ツイスト』（*Oliver Twist*, 1837-39 連載、1838 出版）、『デイヴィッド・コパフィールド』（*David Copperfield*, 1849-50）など多数の作品がある。

Henry James：「ヘンリー・ジェイムズ（1843-1916）」米国生まれで、晩年に英国に帰化した作家。ヨーロッパとアメリカの狭間で揺れ動く人物たちのストーリーを緻密に描き出すことを通じて、同時に小説形式の革新者となった。ニューヨーク版（New York Edition, 1907-09）と呼ばれる自選作品集の各巻に付した序文は、のちに『小説の技巧』（*The Art of the Novel*, 1934）として集成された。『ねじの回転』（*The Turn of the Screw*, 1898）はジェイムズの技巧的洗練が作品の謎を際立たせる効果を発揮する例として広く知られている。

Wuthering Heights：「『嵐が丘』（1847）」長姉シャーロット（Charlotte Brontë, 1816-55）、末妹アン（Anne Brontë, 1820-49）とともにブロンテ姉妹の一人として知られる英国の作家エミリー・ブロンテ（Emily Brontë, 1818-48）の小説。都会から田舎に移住してきたロックウッド（Lockwood）が、家政婦ネリー（Nelly）によって語られた「嵐が丘」をめぐる二つの家の物語を再現して読者に提示する、という形式になっている。

D. H. Lawrence：「D・H・ロレンス（1885-1930）」 ▶ Chapter 15 Sexual Politics

Cinderella：「『シンデレラ』」広くヨーロッパに伝わる民話で、その起源は古代にまで遡るとされる。継母にいじめられていた不遇の少女が、超自然的な力を持った存在の助力で最終的に王子と結婚して王妃になる物語。グリム童話版、ディズニー映画版をはじめとするさまざまな異なるバージョンを通じて世界中に知られている。

The Brothers Grimm：「グリム兄弟」ドイツの文献学者・言語学者・民間伝承研究者。兄ヤーコプ（Jacob Grimm, 1785-1863）、弟ヴィルヘルム（Wilhelm Grimm, 1786-1859）の二人で協力して童話を集成し出版した。

Walt Disney：「ウォルト・ディズニー（1901-66）」米国の映画制作者。ミッキーマウス（Mickey Mouse）やドナルド・ダック（Donald Duck）を主人公にした短編映画で人気を博し、世界初のカラー長編アニメ『白雪姫』（*Show White and the Seven Dwarfs*, 1937）を制作した、アニメーション映画の革新者。数々のヒット作品の中には、『シンデレラ』（*Cinderella*, 1950）をはじめ古今東西の昔話

をリメイクしたものも多い。

Sophocles：「ソフォクレス（496–406BC 頃）」古代ギリシアの三大悲劇詩人のひとり。『オイディプス王』（*Oedipus Rex*）は、それと知らずに王である父を殺して自身の母と結婚したテーバイの王オイディプスの悲劇を描く物語であり、精神分析における「エディプス・コンプレックス」（Oedipus complex ▶ Chapter 2 Ambiguity）の概念の由来となった。

Walter Benjamin：「ヴァルター・ベンヤミン（1892–1940）」ドイツの哲学者・批評家・社会思想家。マルクス主義歴史哲学の影響を受けながらも、独自の思想と文章で近代の意味を問い続けた。「複製技術時代の芸術作品」（'Das Kunstwerk im Zeitalter seiner technischen Reproduzierbarkeit', 1935）、『パサージュ論』（*Passagenwerk*, 1940）などの著作で知られる。

J. D. Salinger：「J・D・サリンジャー（1919–2010）」米国の作家。代表作『ライ麦畑でつかまえて』（*The Catcher in the Rye*, 1951）は今なお世界中の若者たちの心をとらえ続ける青春小説として名高い。

60 Years Later: Coming Through the Rye：「『60 年後──ライ麦畑を通り抜けて』（2009）」スウェーデンの編集者フレデリック・コルティング（Frederik Colting）が J・D・カリフォルニア（J. D. California）の筆名で出版した、『ライ麦畑でつかまえて』の主人公ホールデン・コールフィールドの60 年後の姿を描いた小説。

解説

implied author：「内包された作者」ナラトロジーの用語。現実の作者自身とは異なり、あくまで作品に書かれた言葉から想定される像として作品の「中にいる＝内包された」作者のこと。この概念を導入することにより、「現実の作者が実際に何を意図していたか（あるいはいなかったか）」という問いとは別の問題として、「作品そのものから読み取れる作者の意図」を論じることができる。

narratology：「ナラトロジー」物語構造や叙述形式から作品を分析・分類する文学研究の一分野。民話の構造分析をおこなったロシアのウラジーミル・プロップ（Vladimir Propp, 1895–1970）の業績が構造主義（▶ Chapter 12 Structuralism）の批評家たちによって再発見されたのをきっかけに発展した。

implied reader：「内包された読者」ナラトロジーの用語。「内包された作者」と同様に、現実の読者一人ひとりとは異なる、あくまで作品によって読み手として想定されている作品内読者像のこと。

unreliable narrator：「信頼できない語り手」ナラトロジーの用語。語り手の言動の正当性・信憑性に対して読者の疑いの念を引き起こさせようという内包された作者の意図が読み取れる場合、その語り手を「信頼できない語り手」と呼ぶ。デイヴィッド・ロッジ（▶ Chapter 13 Deconstruction）によれば、信頼できない語り手を用いることで、見せかけと現実のギャップや、人間というものがいかに現実を歪めたり隠したりする存在であるかということを、印象的な形で明らかにできる。『ねじの回転』の語り手は、信頼できない語り手の最も有名で印象的な例のひとつとされている。

Chapter 4: Epic

作家・(登場) 人物・作品リスト

Beowulf:「『ベーオウルフ』」8 世紀に書かれたとされる作者不詳の英国最古の英雄叙事詩。古代スカンディ
ナヴィアの伝説を素材に、英雄ベーオウルフが怪物を退治する武勇物語。

the Grendels:「グレンデル親子」グレンデルは『ベーオウルフ』に出てくる怪物。最終的に主人公ベー
オウルフに退治されるが、作中片腕をもぎ取られた際にその母親が復讐に現れる。

El Cid and Alfonso VI:「エル・シッドとアルフォンソ 6 世」12 世紀後半頃に成立したとされるスペイ
ンの叙事詩『わがシッドの歌』(*The Song of the Cid*) の登場人物。主人公エル・シッドはカスティー
リャ王国の貴族で、アルフォンソ 6 世は王位継承すると共にシッドをカスティーリャから追放する。

W. P. Ker:「W・P・カー (1855–1923)」スコットランドの文学研究者・批評家。著作に『叙事詩とロ
マンス』(*Epic and Romance*, 1897) がある。

John Gardner:「ジョン・ガードナー (1933–82)」米国の小説家で 1971 年に小説『グレンデル』
(*Grendel*) を出版。

Edgar Allan Poe:「エドガー・アラン・ポー (1809–49)」米国ロマン主義を代表する詩人・小説家・
批評家。創作では恐怖と美を統合して独自の世界を生み出した。「アッシャー家の崩壊」('The Fall of
the House of Usher', 1839)、詩「大鴉」('The Raven', 1845) など。

Thomas Hardy:「トマス・ハーディ (1840–1928)」英国の小説家・詩人で、『覇王たち』(*The
Dynasts*, 1904) は本文の通り。代表作は『ダーバヴィル家のテス』(*Tess of the d'Urbervilles*,
1891)。

Iliad:「イーリアス」ホメロス (Homer, 8–9BC 頃) 作とされるトロイ戦争をうたった同名の叙事詩の主
人公。

Napoleon [Bonaparte]:「ナポレオン・ボナパルト (1769–1821)」ナポレオン一世 (在位 1804–
14, 1815) としてフランス第一帝政の皇帝となる。

Maurice Bowra:「モーリス・バウラ (1898–1971)」英国の文学研究者でオックスフォード大学の詩
学教授。『ウェルギリウスからミルトンまで』(*From Virgil to Milton*, 1945) など著書多数。

Tom Clancy:「トム・クランシー (1947–2013)」米国の軍事やスパイをあつかったテクノスリラー小
説を多数執筆。ジャック・ライアン (Jack Ryan) が主人公のシリーズのなかでも、『レッド・オクトー
バーを追え!』(*The Hunt for Red October*, 1984) が代表作。

Andy McNab:「アンディ・マクナブ (1959–)」英国の元軍人で、その経験を下に多数のアクションス
リラー小説を執筆している。

Emily Brontë:「エミリー・ブロンテ (1818–48)」英国の小説家で、代表作は『嵐が丘』(*Wuthering
Heights*, 1847)。ヒースクリフ (Heathcliff) はその主人公。 ▶ Chapter 3 Narrative / Story

Kingsley Amis:「キングズリー・エイミス (1922–95)」英国の小説家で、1950 年代に「怒れる若者
たち」(Angry Young Men) と呼ばれた作家の一人。ジム・ディクソン (Jim Dixon) はエイミスの『ラッ
キー・ジム』(*Lucky Jim*, 1954) の主人公。

Dan Brown:「ダン・ブラウン (1964–)」米国の推理小説家。『ダ・ヴィンチ・コード』(*The Da Vinci*

Code, 2003) が世界的なベストセラーとなる。その小説を含む一連の小説群の主人公が、<u>ロバート・ラングドン（Robert Langdon）</u>。

Gilgamish（別綴り *Gilgamesh*）：「『ギルガメシュ』」古代メソポタミアのウルクの王ギルガメシュを主人公とした英雄叙事詩。「物語の要素はシュメール起源のものが多いが、前1500〜前1000年ごろにアッカド語（バビロニア・アッシリア語諸方言の総称）で編述され、楔形文字粘土書板<ruby>に<rt>くさびがた</rt></ruby>記されて伝えられた」（『世界文学大事典』集英社）。

[John] Milton：「ジョン・ミルトン（1608−74）」 ▶ Chapter 1 Mimesis

Paradise Lost：「『失楽園』（1667, 1674）」 ▶ Chapter 1 Mimesis

[Alexander] Pope：「アレキサンダー・ポープ（1688−1744）」英国の詩人。モック・エピックの『<u>愚物列伝</u>』（<u>*The Dunciad*, 1728−42</u>）や『髪盗人』（*The Rape of the Lock*, 1712, 1714）が有名。

Virgil：「ウェルギリウス（70−19BC）」ローマの詩人。叙事詩『アエネーイス』（*Aeneis*）が有名。

D. W. Griffith：「D・W・グリフィス（1875−1948）」米国の映画監督で、様々な映画技術を確立して、映画芸術の父と呼ばれる。『<u>國民の創生</u>』（<u>*The Birth of a Nation*, 1915</u>）の内容は人種差別的偏見に満ちているが、南北戦争とその後の南部が壮大な叙事詩のように描かれている。

John Wayne：「ジョン・ウェイン（1907−79）」米国の映画俳優。西部劇の名手ジョン・フォード監督（John Ford, 1894−1973）の『駅馬車』（*Stagecoach*, 1939）を皮切りに、主にハリウッドの西部劇でスターとなる。

Saul Bellow：「ソール・ベロー（1915−2005）」ユダヤ系米国人作家で1976年にはノーベル文学賞受賞。

[Lev Nikolayevich] Tolstoy：「レフ・ニコラエヴィチ・トルストイ（1828−1910）」 ▶ Chapter 1 Mimesis

[Marcel] Proust：「マルセル・プルースト（1871−1922）」フランスの小説家で代表作『失われた時を求めて』（*À la recherche du temps perdu*, 1913−27）は20世紀を代表する傑作とされている。

Tom Jones：「『トム・ジョーンズ』」英国の劇作家・小説家ヘンリー・フィールディング（Henry Fielding, 1707−54）（▶ Chapter 3 Narrative / Story）による、捨て子のトムを主人公とした1749年刊の小説で、『散文による喜劇的叙事詩』という彼の小説の理想がこの作で実現された感が深い」（『日本大百科全書』小学館）と訳者でもある朱牟田夏雄は述べている。

Middlemarch：「『ミドルマーチ』」英国の小説家ジョージ・エリオット（George Eliot, 1819−80）による1871−72年の長編小説で、英国の架空の地方都市ミドルマーチを舞台にあらゆる社会階層の人々の人生を交錯させながら、社会描写や人物心理を緻密に描いた作品。

James Joyce：「ジェイムズ・ジョイス（1882−1941）」アイルランドの小説家・詩人で、代表作『<u>ユリシーズ</u>』（<u>*Ulysses*, 1922</u>）は、20世紀を代表する傑作とされ、ホメロスの『オデュッセイア』（▶ Chapter 1 Mimesis）を下敷きに、主人公レオポルド・ブルーム（Leopold Bloom）の1904年6月16日の1日を描いた作品。

Davina McCall：「ダヴィーナ・マッコール（1967−　）」英国の元モデルのTVプレゼンター。

解説

mock-epic：「モック・エピック（擬似英雄詩）」はモック・ヒロイック（mock-heroic）とも言われる文学形式で、卑小な出来事を叙事詩的な英雄や形式を援用しながら詠ずる風刺詩。

Chapter 5: Gothic

作家・（登場）人物・作品リスト

Richard Davenport-Hines：「リチャード・ダヴェンポート＝ハインズ（1953- ）」英国の歴史家、文芸伝記作家。詩人 W・H・オーデン（W. H. Auden, 1907–73）の伝記で知られる。

Edmund Burke：「エドマンド・バーク（1729–97）」アイルランド生まれの政治家・弁論家。著書に『フランス革命についての省察』（*Reflections on the Revolution in France*, 1790）など。

[Sigmund] Freud：「ジークムント・フロイト（1856–1939）」▶ Chapter 2 Ambiguity

'Civilisation and its Discontents'：「「文化への不満」（1930）」フロイト後期の文明批評。

[Georg Wilhelm Fridrich] Hegel：「ゲオルク・ヴィルヘルム・フリードリヒ・ヘーゲル（1770–1831）」ドイツ観念論を代表する哲学者。弁証法で知られる。『精神現象学』（*Phänomenologie des Geistes*, 1807）など。

Grendel's Mother: ▶ Chapter 4 Epic

Dracula：「ドラキュラ伯爵」アイルランド作家ブラム・ストーカー（Bram Stoker, 1847–1912）による『ドラキュラ』（*Dracula*, 1897）の主人公の吸血鬼。

Hannibal Lecter：「ハンニバル・レクター」『羊たちの沈黙』（*The Silence of the Lambs*, 1988）『ハンニバル』（*Hannibal*, 1999）等、米国作家トマス・ハリス（Thomas Harris, 1940- ）の作品に登場する精神科医にして猟奇殺人者。映画版では英国の俳優<u>アンソニー・ホプキンズ（Anthony Hopkins, 1937- ）</u>が演じた。

Mary Shelley：「メアリー・シェリー（1797–1851）」英国の作家。父はフランスの啓蒙思想の影響を受けた作家・哲学者のウィリアム・ゴドウィン（William Godwin, 1756–1836）、母は最初期のフェミニズム運動家としても位置付けられる作家、思想家のメアリ・ウルストンクラフト（Mary Wollstonecraft, 1759–97）。<u>『フランケンシュタインあるいは現代のプロメテウス』（*Frankenstein; or, the Modern Prometheus*, 1818, 1831）</u>はゴシック作品の金字塔。結婚相手はロマン主義詩人のパーシー・ビッシュ・シェリー（Percy Bysshe Shelley, 1792–1822）。

[Denis] Diderot：「ドゥニ・ディドロ（1713–84）」フランスの思想家・小説家。ダランベール（Jean Le Rond d'Alembert, 1717–83）とともに<u>『百科全書』（*Encyclopedie*, 1751–72）</u>を編集した。

Pride and Prejudice and Zombies：「『高慢と偏見とゾンビ』（2009）」米国の作家・映画製作者セス・グレアム＝スミス（Seth Grahame-Smith, 1976- ）による『高慢と偏見』（▶ Chapter 1 Mimesis）のパロディ小説。共著者にオースティン（▶ Chapter 1 Mimesis）の名を掲げている。

Heathcliff：「ヒースクリフ」▶ Chapter 4 Epic

Wuthering Heights：「『嵐が丘』（1847）」▶ Chapter 3 Narrative / Story

Laurence Olivier：「ローレンス・オリヴィエ（1907–89）」英国の俳優・演出家。

Ralph Fiennes：「レイフ・ファインズ（1962- ）」英国の俳優・映画監督・映画製作者。『ハリー・ポッター』（*Harry Potter*）シリーズではヴォルデモート卿を演じた。

Cliff Richard：「クリフ・リチャード（1940- ）」英国の歌手。

James Bond：「ジェイムズ・ボンド」英国作家イアン・フレミング（Ian Fleming, 1908–64）の一連の

スパイ小説における主人公。

Isabella Linton：「イザベラ・リントン」『嵐が丘』（▶ Chapter 3 Narrative / Story）に登場する「スラッシュクロス」屋敷に住むリントン家の次女。兄のエドガーがヒースクリフの恋人キャサリンと結婚したため、ヒースクリフは復讐のためにイザベラと結婚する。

Emily Brontë：▶ Chapter 4 Epic

解説

... as Edmund Burke wrote in 1756：『自然社会の擁護』（*A Vindication of Natural Society*, 1756）での記述。

drive：「欲動」生物や人間の行動を引き起こす内因性の力を指す心理学用語。

Romanticism：「ロマン主義」18 世紀末から 19 世紀前半にかけての西洋で起こった芸術運動。文学においては理性による束縛を嫌い、想像力を自由に用いて情緒豊かに個性を発揮することを重んじた。

the Enlightenment：「啓蒙主義」17 世紀〜 18 世紀の西洋に起こった、人間の理性の尊重に真理と幸福の礎があるとする思想運動。

the classic Victorian novel：『嵐が丘』の発刊年はヴィクトリア朝（1837–1901）であるがその実質は、道徳主義や上品さの尊重、楽観主義を特徴とする「ヴィクトリア朝文学」の枠に収まるものではない。

Byronic：「英国ロマン主義の詩人バイロン［George Gordon Byron, 1788–1824］の詩（に出てくる美男の主人公）のように悲壮でロマンティックでもの憂わし気な」

Chapter 6: Culture

作家・（登場）人物・作品リスト

T. S. Eliot：「T・S・エリオット（1888-1965）」『文化の定義のための覚書』(*Notes Towards the Definition of Culture*, 1948) を含む評論も数多く執筆。▶ Chapter 2 Ambiguity

Matthew Arnold：「マシュー・アーノルド（1822-88）」英国の詩人であり、文化批評家。著作『教養と無秩序』(*Culture and Anarchy*, 1869) で知られる。

Goethe：「ゲーテ（1749-1832）」ロマン主義時代のドイツの代表的文豪。戯曲『ファウスト』(*Faust*, 1808, 1832) や小説『若きウェルテルの悩み』(*Die Leiden des jungen Werthers*, 1774) が有名。

James Baldwin：「ジェイムズ・ボールドウィン（1924-87）」米国のアフリカ系作家。人種やセクシュアリティを主題とした作品が多い。'Stranger in the Village'（「村のよそ者」、1953）は、滞在先のスイスで唯一の黒人として感じた疎外感を、母国アメリカで黒人として抱く疎外感に接続して語ったエッセイ。

Dante [Alighieri]：「ダンテ・アリギエーリ（1265-1321）」イタリアの詩人。叙事詩『神曲』(*La Divina Commedia*, 1307-21) が有名。ダンテ以下の人名は、ボールドウィンのエッセイ中ではヨーロッパの有名芸術家の例として登場。

[William] Shakespeare：「ウィリアム・シェイクスピア（1564-1616）」▶ Chapter 2 Ambiguity

Michelangelo：「ミケランジェロ（1475-1564）」ルネサンス期イタリアの芸術家。彫刻、絵画、建築、詩など多様な作品を残す。

Aeschylus：「アイスキュロス（525-456BC 頃）」古代ギリシアの三大悲劇詩人のひとり。『アガメムノン』(*Agamemnon*) が代表作。

[Leonardo] Da Vinci：「レオナルド・ダ・ヴィンチ（1452-1519）」ミケランジェロと並ぶルネサンス期イタリア最大の芸術家・科学者。絵画『モナ・リザ』(*La Gioconda*, 1503-06 頃) ほか、多様な分野に業績がある。

Rembrandt [van Rijn]：「レンブラント・ファン・レイン（1606-69）」オランダの画家。光と陰のコントラストを強調した技法を使う。

Racine：「ジャン・バティスト・ラシーヌ（1639-99）」フランス古典主義時代の劇作家。『フェードル』(*Phèdre*, 1677) など、古代ギリシア、ローマを題材にした悲劇で知られる。

Beethoven：「ベートーヴェン（1770-1827）」ドイツの作曲家、ピアニスト。古典派からロマン主義音楽への道を開いた。

Bach：「バッハ（1685-1750）」ドイツ出身のバロック音楽の代表的作曲家。近代西洋音楽の基礎を確立した存在として知られる。

D. H. Lawrence：「D・H・ロレンス（1885-1930）」▶ Chapter 15 Sexual Politics

Lady Chatterley：「チャタレイ夫人」▶ Chapter 15 Sexual Politics

Lionel Trilling：「ライオネル・トリリング（1905-75)」米国の批評家。『文化を超えて』(*Beyond Culture: Essays on Literature and Learning*, 1965) などの著作において、文化や歴史が文学作品に与える影響を重視した。

Richard Hoggart：「リチャード・ホガート（1918-2014)」英国の批評家。『読み書き能力の効能』(*The Uses of Literacy: Aspects of Working-Class Life*, 1957) で、マスメディアの到来が大衆文化に変化をもたらすさまを活写し、メディア・スタディーズやカルチュラル・スタディーズの先駆となった。

Danielle Steel：「ダニエル・スティール（1947-　)」米国の作家。ロマンス小説を数多く発表し、しばしばベストセラーになった。

Allan Bloom：「アラン・ブルーム（1930-92)」米国の思想家。『アメリカン・マインドの終焉——文化と教育の危機』(*The Closing of American Mind: How Higher Education Has Failed Democracy and Impoverished the Souls of Today's Students*, 1987) において、アメリカの大学教育における価値相対主義の蔓延が批判的思考力を低下させ精神の閉塞につながると説いた。

解説

Barbarians; Philistines; Populace：「野蛮人、ペリシテ人、大衆」それぞれ、アーノルド『教養と無秩序』の第三章のタイトルに使われているキーワードで、文化の大衆化を招く元凶のような存在。

sweetness and light：「甘美と光」『教養と無秩序』においてアーノルドは、美や知性を象徴する「甘美と光」こそ文化のなかでもっとも価値のあるものだと主張している。

Cultural Studies：「カルチュラル・スタディーズ、文化研究」20 世紀後半に英国の研究者たちにより始まった。マルクス主義の影響下に既存のアカデミズムに対する批判的考察を加え、従来研究対象とされてこなかったサブカルチャーの諸相を扱うことを特徴とする。

Cultural Wars：「文化戦争、保守主義者と自由主義者の価値観の衝突」1991 年出版のジェイムズ・デイヴィスン・ハンター（James Davison Hunter, 1955-　) の同名の著書でクローズアップされた、人種、ジェンダー、環境などさまざまな事象についての政策をめぐる文化的グループ間の対立を指す。

Chapter 7: Base / Superstructure

作家・（登場）人物・作品リスト

George Orwell：「ジョージ・オーウェル（1903–50）」▶ Chapter 1 Mimesis

The Road to Wigan Pier：「『ウィガン波止場への道』（1937）」恐慌期の英国北部の炭鉱地帯への取材と自伝的散文を通じて社会主義の価値を問う Orwell の著作。

Bertolt Brecht：「ベルトルト・ブレヒト（1898–1956）」▶ Chapter 1 Mimesis

[Karl] Marx：「カール・マルクス（1818–83）」ドイツの思想家、経済学者、革命家。唯物史観に基づく思想を展開し、フリードリヒ・エンゲルス（Friedrich Engels, 1820–95）とともに社会・経済、政治を統べる社会主義理論を発展させる。代表的著作に『共産党宣言』（*Manifest der Kommunistischen Partei*, エンゲルスとの共著、1848）、『資本論』（*Das Kapital*, 1867–94）。文中で引用されている下部構造、上部構造のくだりは、『経済学批判』（*A Contribution to the Critique of Political Economy*, 1859）の「序言」からの一節。

Avatar：「『アバター』」2009 年公開のジェームズ・キャメロン監督（Francis Cameron, 1954– ）による米国映画。最新技術を駆使した３D 映像が話題となった。

Robinson Crusoe：「『ロビンソン・クルーソー』（1719）」風刺的作風で知られる英国の作家ダニエル・デフォー（Daniel Defoe, 1660–1731）による小説。タイトルと同名の船乗りの主人公が無人島に漂着して生きのびるさまを描く。▶ Chapter 11 Metafiction

Hamlet：『ハムレット』▶ Chapter 2 Ambiguity

H. G. Wells：「H・G・ウェルズ（1866–1946）」英国出身の SF 黎明期の代表的作家。国際連盟の樹立を提唱するなど幅広い社会活動も行なった。作品に『タイム・マシン』（*The Time Machine*, 1895）、『透明人間』（*The Invisible Man*, 1897）、『宇宙戦争』（*The War of the Worlds*, 1898）など。

George Gissing：「ジョージ・ギッシング（1857–1903）」英国の作家。優秀な学生として将来を約束されながら 17 歳の少女と出会い、売春から救い更生させる過程で人生が変わる。『暁の労働者たち』（*Workers in the Dawn*, 1880）は、後に最初の妻となるその少女との生活をもとに、労働者階級を自然主義的に描いた小説第１作。

Sophocles：「ソフォクレス（496–406BC 頃）」▶ Chapter 3 Narrative/Story

Aristotle：「アリストテレス（384–322BC）」▶ Chapter 1 Mimesis

Oedipus Rex：「『オイディプス王』」▶ Chapter 3 Narrative/Story

解説

Marxist：「マルクス主義の」マルクス主義は、マルクスとエンゲルスによって発展された社会主義思想体系。その諸概念は人文科学の領域でもしばしば参照される。

Base/superstructure：「下部構造／上部構造」『経済学批判』でマルクスが提示した、土台となる経済

構造（下部構造）が、法、政治、道徳、芸術、宗教などその他の社会的側面（上部構造）を決定するという考え。

'Erst fressen!' ('Grub comes first!')：ドイツ語原文は、正しくは Erst kommt das Fressen, dann kommt die Mora となる。ブレヒトの代表作『三文オペラ』（*Die Dreigroshenoper,* 1928）からの引用で、「食うのが先だ。道徳は後回し」の意。

surplus value：「剰余価値」マルクス主義経済学の基本概念で、労働者の必要な労働を超えて生み出される労働力に与えられる価値。これが資本家により搾取されることで、利益が生まれる。

homo economicus：「経済人、ホモ・エコノミクス」経済学に現れる、もっぱら経済的合理的にのみ基づいて行動するとされる人間像。

New Marxists：「新マルクス主義者」Neo Marxists とも。社会学、精神分析、批評理論など他分野の知見を取り入れつつ、ヘルベルト・マルクーゼ（Herbert Marcuse, 1898-1979）らのフランクフルト学派を起点に、20世紀を通じてマルクス主義思想を拡大しようと試みた人々を指す。

Chapter 8: The Canon

作家・(登場) 人物・作品リスト

[William] Shakespeare：「ウィリアム・シェイクスピア（1564–1616）」 ▶ Chapter 2 Ambiguity

Virginia Woolf：「ヴァージニア・ウルフ（1882–1941）」英国の作家、批評家。知的、芸術的家庭環境に育ち、ブルームズベリ・グループと呼ばれる文学者、芸術家、思想家の集まりの中心的な役割を果たす。『ダロウェイ夫人』（*Mrs Dalloway*, 1925）、『灯台へ』（*To the Lighthouse*, 1927）など、「意識の流れ」の手法を用いたモダニズム文学の代表的作品を残した。

H. G. Wells：「H・G・ウェルズ（1866–1946）」 ▶ Chapter 7 Base / Superstructure

Theodore Dreiser：「シオドア・ドライサー（1871–1945）」米国の小説家。急速な産業化と都市化の進展する世紀転換期アメリカの社会的現実を背景に人間の欲望のありさまを描いた、米国の自然主義文学を代表する作家。主な作品に『シスター・キャリー』（*Sister Carrie*, 1900）、『ジェニー・ゲアハート』（*Jennie Gerhardt*, 1911）、『アメリカの悲劇』（*An American Tragedy*, 1925）などがある。

Rebecca West：「レベッカ・ウェスト（1892–1983）」英国の小説家、批評家、ジャーナリスト。フェミニズムと社会主義の立場から積極的な発言と行動を続け、数々のノンフィクションを著した。女性による初の第一次世界大戦をめぐる小説『兵士の帰還』（*The Return of the Soldier*, 1918）や、ナチスの戦争犯罪を裁く国際軍事裁判であるニュルンベルク裁判のルポタージュなどで知られる。

[Matthew] Arnold：「マシュー・アーノルド（1822–88）」 ▶ Chapter 6 Culture

[Geoffrey] Chaucer：「ジェフリー・チョーサー（1343頃–1400）」中世イングランドの代表的詩人。カンタベリー大聖堂に参詣する巡礼者たちの24編の物語からなる散文をまじえた韻文説話集『カンタベリー物語』（*The Canterbury Tales*, 1387–1400）を著した。「学僧（The Clerk）」が語るのは、イタリアの侯爵が妻の自分への愛を試そうとさまざまな奇策を講じる物語。

Samuel Johnson：「サミュエル・ジョンソン（1709–84）」英国の文献学者、批評家、詩人。『英語辞典』（*A Dictionary of the English Language*, 1755）、『シェイクスピア全集』（*The Plays of William Shakespeare*, 1765）、『詩人列伝』（*Lives of the Most Eminent Poets*, 1779–81）などの編纂を通じて英文学のキャノン形成に大きく寄与した、18世紀英国における文壇の大御所。

Methuselah：「メトシェラ」旧約聖書の『創世記』に登場する人物で、ノアの祖父。ノアの洪水以前の族長で、969歳まで生きたとされる。

Moby-Dick：「『白鯨』（1851）」米国の小説家・詩人ハーマン・メルヴィル（Herman Melville, 1819–91）の長大な小説。巨大な白鯨モービー・ディックを追跡する船長エイハブと乗組員たちの冒険譚であると同時に、神への懐疑と挑戦の結果敗れ去る人間の悲劇を描いた物語であり、しばしばアメリカ文学を代表する作品のひとつに数えられる。

Hamlet：『ハムレット』 ▶ Chapter 2 Ambiguity

Hard Times：「『ハード・タイムズ』（1854）」英国の小説家チャールズ・ディケンズ（Charles Dickens ▶ Chapter 3 Narrative / Story）の小説。

Silas Marner：「『サイラス・マーナー』（1861）」英国の小説家ジョージ・エリオット（George Eliot,

1819–80）の小説。

Tess of the d'Urbervilles：「『ダーバヴィル家のテス』（1891）」英国の小説家トマス・ハーディ（Thomas Hardy, 1840–1928）の小説。

Jane Eyre：「『ジェーン・エア』（1847）」 ▶ Chapter 15 Sexual Politics

War and Peace：「『戦争と平和』（1865–69）」 ▶ Chapter 4 Epic

Napoleon [Bonaparte]：「ナポレオン・ボナパルト（1769–1821）」 ▶ Chapter 4 Epic

[Lev Nikolayevich] Tolstoy：「レフ・ニコラエヴィチ・トルストイ（1828–1910）」 ▶ Chapter 1 Mimesis

解説

canon wars：「正典論争」1980–90 年代に巻き起こった、人文学のキャノンをめぐる対立と論争。1960 年代以降、主に人種、ジェンダー、階級という視点からキャノンの見直しと多様化が進んできたのに対し、哲学者アラン・ブルーム（Allan Bloom, 1930–92）や文学批評家ハロルド・ブルーム（Harold Bloom, 1930–2019）らは伝統的な西洋人文学の正典を保持することを主張した。

canon-making/canonisation：「正典化」ある特定の作品群を、誰もが読むべき価値のある正典として認定すること。

Chapter 9: Genre

作家・（登場）人物・作品リスト

Margaret Atwood：「マーガレット・アトウッド（1939–　）」カナダの小説家、詩人。『侍女の物語』（*The Handmaid's Tale*, 1985）は SF 的な設定を持つ小説で、数々の賞を受賞した。

[Isaac] Asimov：「アイザック・アシモフ（1920–92）」米国の作家で、SF の大家。小説の中で提唱した「ロボット工学三原則」でも知られる。

[Chinua] Achebe：「チヌア・アチェベ（1930–2013）」ナイジェリアの小説家、詩人。著作に『崩れゆく絆』（*Things Fall Apart*, 1958）など。

S. S. Van Dine：「Ｓ・Ｓ・ヴァン・ダイン（1888–1939）」米国の推理作家。本名ウィラード・ハンティントン・ライト（Willard Huntington Wright）。

Robert Traver：「ロバート・トレイヴァー（1903–91）」法廷ものを得意とした米国の作家で、法律家でもあった。代表作は、映画化もされた『錯乱』（*Anatomy of a Murder*, 1958）。

John Grisham：「ジョン・グリシャム（1955–　）」米国の作家。数々のベストセラーを生み出している。

Alfred Hitchcock：「アルフレッド・ヒッチコック（1899–1980）」英国の映画監督。サスペンス映画を多く撮った。その作風と映画技法は後の映画監督に大きな影響力を持つ。

Georgette Heyer：「ジョージェット・ヘイヤー（1902–74）」英国の作家で、摂政時代を舞台とした「リージェンシー・ロマンス」（Regency romance）の創始者。

Edgar Allan Poe：「エドガー・アラン・ポー（1809–49）」 ▶ Chapter 4 Epic

Hugo Gernsback：「ヒューゴー・ガーンズバック（1884–1967）」米国の作家、編集者。ＳＦの発展に寄与した。

Galaxy Quest：「『ギャラクシー・クエスト』（1999）」米国の映画で、2000 年度ヒューゴー賞受賞作。架空のＳＦテレビシリーズを核とした物語で、コンヴェンションに集まるファンの姿も描かれる。

Barbara Cartland：「バーバラ・カートランド（1901–2000）」英国のベストセラー作家。1 年間の小説出版数でギネス世界記録を持つ。

Aristotle：「アリストテレス（384–322BC）」 ▶ Chapter 1 Mimesis

Stephen King：「スティーヴン・キング（1947–　）」ホラーをはじめとする様々なジャンルでヒット作を生み出している米国の作家。映像化された作品も多い。「ガンスリンガー」・サーガ（'Gunslinger' saga）は正式には『ダーク・タワー』（*The Dark Tower*, 1982–2004）というタイトルの全 7 部構成の長編小説。

Henry James：「ヘンリー・ジェイムズ（1843–1916）」米国生まれの小説家で、後に英国に帰化。「メイジーの知ったこと」（*What Maisie Knew*, 1897）は夫婦の離婚劇を娘のメイジーの視点を通じて描く。 ▶ Chapter 3 Narrative / Story

Salman Rushdie：「サルマン・ラシュディ（1947–　）」インド出身の英国の小説家。『真夜中の子供たち』（*Midnight's Children*, 1981）は主人公の子供時代の話が本人の視点から語られる。主人公はテレパシー

能力で遠くの子供たちと言葉や文化の壁さえも超えてコミュニケーションをとることができる。

John Wyndham：「ジョン・ウィンダム（1903-69）」英国のＳＦ作家。『呪われた村』(*Village of the Damned* [*The Midwich Cuckoos*], 1957) では、宇宙人の「托卵」により生まれテレパシー能力を持つ子供たちが登場する。

A. S. Byatt：「Ａ・Ｓ・バイアット（1936-　）」英国の小説家、詩人。『抱擁』(*Possession: A Romance*, 1990) は英国の権威ある文学賞、ブッカー賞を受賞した。

Paul Auster：「ポール・オースター（1947-　）」現代アメリカを代表する小説家の一人。『ガラスの街』(*City of Glass*, 1985) で使われるウィリアム・ウィルソン（William Wilson）という名前は、ポーの同名短編小説の主人公の名前でもある。

Jacques Derrida：「ジャック・デリダ（1930-2004）」 ▶ Chapter 13 Deconstruction

解説

a Hugo and a Nebula：「ヒューゴー賞とネビュラ賞」アメリカの二大ＳＦ賞。前者はファン投票によって選ばれ、後者は作家らの投票によって選ばれる。

the Edgar：「エドガー賞」アメリカ探偵作家クラブ（Mystery Writers of America）が主催する、アメリカで出版された優れた推理小説に与えられる賞。クラブのロゴには賞の名前にもなっているポーの顔が使われている。

Worldcon (World Science Fiction Convention)：「ワールドコン（世界ＳＦ大会）」1939 年から開かれている大規模なＳＦ大会。ヒューゴー賞の投票と発表はこの大会中に行われる。

Russian formalists：「ロシア・フォルマリズム」（Russian formalism）は 1910 年代から 30 年代ロシアにおける文学批評の一派で、文学作品の形式や手法に着目した。

magic realism：「マジックリアリズム」元々は 20 世紀前半の美術の用語だったが文学批評にも取り入れられ、現在ではラテンアメリカ文学などの非西洋文学に適用されることが多い。リアリズムの中に非現実的な要素が混じりこむことが特徴とされる。

hard-boiled：「ハードボイルド」1920 年代アメリカにはじまった、探偵小説の一ジャンル。従来の、知的な探偵による謎解きをメインにした推理小説に対し、行動的な探偵を主人公に据え人物や社会をよりリアルに描いた。代表的なハードボイルド作家に、ダシール・ハメット（Samuel Dashiell Hammett, 1894-1961）、レイモンド・チャンドラー（Raymond Chandler, 1888-1959）らがいる。

degenerescence：「頽廃」ジャンル（genre）と同じ語源から派生したこの語を、デリダは「ジャンルの掟」（1980）の中でジャンルの境界の不可避的な揺らぎを示すために用いた。

Chapter 10: Allegory

作家・（登場）人物・作品リスト

Plato：▶ Chapter 1 Mimesis

[*The*] *Republic*：▶ Chapter 1 Mimesis

Socrates：「ソクラテス（470頃–399BC）」古代ギリシアの哲学者。「無知の知」に哲学と人間存在の根源を見た。彼自身の著作はなく、弟子のクセノフォン（Xenophon, 430頃–355頃BC）やプラトンの著作によってその思想が伝えられる。

Glaucon：「グラウコン（445頃–400BC）」プラトンの兄。

Jonah：「ヨナ」旧約聖書『ヨナ書』中のヘブライの預言者。嵐を鎮めるために海に放り込まれるが大魚（鯨）に呑み込まれ、三日後陸上に吐き出された。

[Arthur] Schopenhaur：「アルトゥール・ショーペンハウアー（1788–1860）」ドイツの哲学者。主著に『意志と表象としての世界』（*Die Welt als Wille und Vorstellung*, 1818, 1844）など。『余録と補遺』（*Parerga und Paralipomena*, 1851）に収められた「宗教について──ある対話」（'Über Religion'）（本章では *The Horror and Absurdities of Religion*（『宗教の恐ろしさと愚かしさについて』）の一部とされている）はデモフェーレス（Demopheles）とフィラレーテス（Philalethes）の対話篇である。デモフェーレスは大衆にとっての宗教の役割を認め、フィラレーテスは宗教そのものを否定する。

Dorothea Brooke：『ミドルマーチ』の主人公。▶ Chapter 4 Epic

Country Life：「『カントリー・ライフ』」田舎暮らしを扱う1897年創刊の英国の週刊誌。

Kenneth Grahame：「ケネス・グレアム（1859–1932）」英国の児童文学作家。『たのしい川べ』の邦訳で知られる *The Wind in the Willows*（1908）は川ネズミ、モグラ、ヒキガエル、アナグマなどの牧歌的生活を寓意を込めて描く。

H. G. Wells：H・G・ウェルズ（1866–1946）▶ Chapter 7 Base / Superstructure

The War of the Worlds：『宇宙戦争』（1898）▶ Chapter 7 Base / Superstructure

Dr Jekyll and Mr Hyde：「『ジキル博士とハイド氏の奇妙な事例』（*The Strange Case of Dr Jekyll and Mr Hyde*, 1886）」スティーヴンソン（Robert Louis Stevenson, 1850–94）による怪奇小説。

[Sigmund] Freud：「ジークムント・フロイト（1856–1939）」▶ Chapter 2 Ambiguity

Oscar Wilde：「オスカー・ワイルド（Oscar Wilde, 1854–1900」▶ Chapter 2 Ambiguity

Dorian Gray：「『ドリアン・グレイの肖像』（*The Picture of Dorian Gray*, 1891）」のこと。ワイルドの代表作。美貌の青年ドリアン・グレイが悪行を重ねるにつれ、屋根裏に隠した彼の肖像画が醜くなってゆく。

解説

Platonic image：「プラトン的イメージ」プラトン思想の根幹をなすイデア論では、人間は事物の真の存在（イデア）には到達しえないが、そのイメージは共有しているとされる。

the enslavement of the Israelites in the bowels of Egypt：旧約聖書『創世記』に現れるヨセフの子孫（イスラエル人）はエジプトで繁栄するがそれを恐れたエジプト人は彼らを奴隷化して虐げる。そこで『出エジプト記』に示されるように、モーセが彼らを率いてエジプトを脱出する。

The financial catastrophe that ravaged the Western world in 2009：米国発のいわゆるリーマン・ショックに引き続いて、2009年のヨーロッパではギリシア財政の粉飾が明らかとなり、各国に経済危機が連鎖していった。

the recent 'discovery' of canals on Mars：19世紀末、天文学者のジョヴァンニ・スキャパレッリ（Giovanni Virginio Schiaparelli, 1835–1910）やパーシヴァル・ローウェル（Percival Lowell, 1855–1916）によって行われた、火星表面に運河が観察されたとする主張。今日ではその存在は否定されている。

the unconscious self that, in Vienna, Freud was beginning to make sense of：フロイトは神経学者ジャン＝マルタン・シャルコー（Jean-Martin Charcot, 1825–93）のもとで学んだパリ留学からウィーンへ戻ったのちに開業し、1890年代半ばから本格的に精神分析理論を展開してゆく。

'love that dare not speak its name'：ワイルドの恋人だったアルフレッド・ダグラス卿（Lord Alfred Bruce Douglas, 1870–1945）が詩「二つの愛」（'Two Loves', 1892）で同性間の愛を指してあらわした句。

Chapter 11: Metafiction

作家・（登場）人物・作品リスト

Don Quixote：「『ドン・キホーテ』」スペインの作家セルバンテス（Miguel de Cervantes Saavedra, 1547–1616）の小説。前編は 1605 年、後編は 1615 年に刊行された。騎士道物語を読みすぎた郷士アロンソ・キハーノが、自らを騎士と妄想するに至って遍歴の旅に出かける冒険物語。数々の滑稽なエピソードを通じて中世騎士道ロマンスを徹底的に風刺し、近代小説の出発点となった。

The Song of the Cid：「『わがシッドの歌』」▶ Chapter 4 Epic

Henry Fielding：「ヘンリー・フィールディング（1707–54）」▶ Chapter 3 Narrative / Story

Samuel Richardson：「サミュエル・リチャードソン（1689–1761）」▶ Chapter 3 Narrative / Story

Michael Cunningham：「マイケル・カニンガム（1952– ）」米国の小説家。ヴァージニア・ウルフの『ダロウェイ夫人』を下敷きにした小説『めぐりあう時間たち』(*The Hours*, 1998) でピュリッツァー賞とペン／フォークナー賞を受賞した。

Virginia Woolf：「ヴァージニア・ウルフ（1882–1941）」▶ Chapter 8 The Canon

Alexander Pope：「アレキサンダー・ポープ（1688–1744）」▶ Chapter 4 Epic

J. M. Coetzee：「J・M・クッツェー（1952– ）」南アフリカ出身の小説家。『マイケル・K』(*Life and Times of Michael K*, 1983) および『恥辱』(*Disgrace*, 1999) で史上初の二度のブッカー賞受賞、2003 年にはノーベル文学賞を受賞した、現代の英語文学を代表する作家の一人。『敵あるいはフォー』(*Foe*) は 1986 年の作品。

Robinson Crusoe：「ロビンソン・クルーソー」▶ Chapter 7 Base / Superstructure

Laurence Sterne：「ロレンス・スターン（1713–68）」英国の小説家、牧師。近代小説勃興期である 18 世紀イギリスを代表する作品のひとつでありながら散文ジャンルの型を次々に破っていく『トリストラム・シャンディ』(*The Life and Opinions of Tristram Shandy, Gentleman*, 1759–67) の作者として知られる。

Donald Barthelme：「ドナルド・バーセルミ（1931–89）」米国の作家。不安に満ちた不条理な現代世界を遊び心たっぷりに描く、実験精神に富んだ数々の短編作品で知られる。ディズニー映画のグロテスクなパロディとも言える中編小説『雪白姫』(*Snow White*, 1967) も代表作のひとつである。

Robert Graves：「ロバート・グレイヴス（1895–1985）」英国の詩人、小説家、文学研究者。ディケンズの名作を元にした『真のデイヴィッド・コパフィールド』(*The Real David Copperfield*) は 1933 年の作品。

Wuthering Heights：「『嵐が丘』（1847）」▶ Chapter 3 Narrative / Story

Jane Eyre：「『ジェーン・エア』（1847）」▶ Chapter 15 Sexual Politics

Jean Rhys：「ジーン・リース（1890–1979）」英国領ドミニカ出身の小説家。1920–30 年代にかけてヨーロッパを舞台にした作品を発表したのち、約 30 年の沈黙を経て、『ジェーン・エア』の大胆な書き直し

を図った作品『サルガッソーの広い海』(*Wide Sargasso Sea*, 1966) で注目を浴びる。

Andrew Davies：「アンドリュー・デイヴィス (1936–)」英国の小説家。さまざまな代表的ヴィクトリア朝小説を素材に作品を執筆している。

Middlemarch：「『ミドルマーチ』(1871–72)」 ▶ Chapter 4 Epic

[Anthony] Trollope：「アンソニー・トロロープ (1815–82)」英国の小説家。当時の金融スキャンダルを題材に執筆した風刺小説『当世の生き方』(*The Way We Live Now*, 1875) などが代表作とされる。そのほかに、現実にはない架空の州バーセットシアを設定して書いた一連の小説群でも知られている。

[Charles] Dickens：「チャールズ・ディケンズ (1812–70)」 ▶ Chapter 3 Narrative / Story

[Elizabeth] Gaskell：「エリザベス・ギャスケル (1810–65)」英国の小説家。代表作に『メアリー・バートン』(*Mary Barton*, 1848)、『クランフォード』(*Cranford*, 1853) などがある。『ジェーン・エア』の作者シャーロット・ブロンテの伝記を書いてその功績を後世に伝えたことでも有名。

Vanity Fair：「『虚栄の市』(1847–48)」インド生まれの英国の作家サッカレー (William Makepeace Thackeray, 1811–63) の小説。当時の上流・中流階級の生活を写実的・風刺的に描いた、ヴィクトリア朝小説を代表する作品のひとつ。

Tom Brown's Schooldays：「『トム・ブラウンの学校生活』(1857)」英国の作家トマス・ヒューズ (Thomas Hughes, 1822–96) の小説。1830 年代イギリスのパブリック・スクールを舞台に、主人公トム・ブラウンの成長過程を描く。いじめっ子上級生フラッシュマン (Harry Flashman) は敵役でありながら生き生きと描かれ、以後さまざまな小説や映画などで取り上げられる人気キャラクターとなった。

George MacDonald Fraser：「ジョージ・マクドナルド・フレイザー (1925–2008)」英国の小説家、映画脚本家。『トム・ブラウンの学校生活』に登場するハリー・フラッシュマンを題材にした「フラッシュマン」シリーズ ('Flashman' series) と呼ばれる一連の作品を発表し、その映画版『ローヤル・フラッシュ』(*Royal Flash*, 1975) では自ら脚本を執筆した。

Jasper Fforde：「ジャスパー・フォード (1961–)」英国の小説家。古典文学の世界の中に入り込んで原作の物語を変えようとする凶悪犯と戦う「文学刑事サーズデイ・ネクスト」シリーズ ('Thursday Next' series) がベストセラーになる。2003 年出版の *The Well of Lost Plots* (邦訳タイトルは『だれがゴドーを殺したの？』) はシリーズ第 3 作。

A. S. Byatt：「A・S・バイアット (1936–)」 ▶ Chapter 9 Genre

John Fowles：「ジョン・ファウルズ (1926–2005)」英国の小説家。『フランス軍中尉の女』(*The French Lieutenant's Woman*, 1969) はイギリス文学におけるメタフィクションの代表作のひとつとして知られる。

Sarah Waters：「サラ・ウォーターズ (1966–)」英国の小説家。ヴィクトリア朝を舞台にしたミステリー小説で知られる。代表作に『荊の城』(*Fingersmith*, 2002) がある。

解説

parody：「パロディ」他の作品の形式や内容をコミカルなやり方で模倣すること。風刺や批判の意味が込

められることが多いが、かならずしも否定的な意図のみによるものとはかぎらない。

homage：「オマージュ」もともとはヨーロッパの封建社会で領主に対して忠誠の儀式をおこなうこと。転じて文学においては、先行する作品や作家に敬意を表して類似する作品を創作すること。

mock-epic：「擬似英雄詩」取るに足らない些細な出来事をあたかも古代の叙事詩のようなスタイルを模して意図的に仰々しく誇張する風刺詩。ポープの『髪盗人』（*The Rape of the Lock*, 1712–14）はその代表例。▶ Chapter 4 Epic

narcissism：「自己愛、ナルシシズム」泉に映った自分の姿に恋い焦がれて死んだギリシア神話のナルキッソスの物語を由来とする語。フロイト（▶ Chapter 2 Ambiguity）はナルシシズムを自己保存の本能に基づいて自分自身を性的欲望の対象とする精神のメカニズムと捉えた。現在では広く自己陶酔的志向を意味する語として使われている。メタフィクションをナルシシズムという観点から考察した著作にカナダの批評家リンダ・ハッチオン（Linda Hutcheon, 1947– ）の『ナルシス的物語――メタフィクションのパラドックス』（*Narcissistic Narrative: The Metafictional Paradox*, 1980）がある。

self-referentiality：「自己言及性」作品内で語り手が語り手自身、あるいは作品自身に言及すること。それにより、「語っている存在」と「語られている存在」とのあいだで矛盾が生じることがある。その例として、「私は嘘つきです」という文が生じさせる「嘘つきのパラドックス」がよく知られている。

metanarrative：「メタナラティヴ」ある物語全体を統御している高次の観念のこと。『ドン・キホーテ』を例にとれば、「妄想に取りつかれた自称騎士の滑稽な冒険譚」がナラティヴだとすれば、「中世騎士道ロマンスの風刺」というのがメタナラティヴにあたる。

burlesque：「バーレスク」真面目な主題を意図的に軽薄に扱ったり、逆に取るに足らない主題を意図的に深刻ぶって扱ったりすることにより笑いを誘うようなスタイルの作品。

Booker Prize：「ブッカー賞」1969 年に創設された英国の文学賞。2014 年以降は、英語で書かれて英国で出版されたすべての小説を対象に、年に一度受賞作が決定されている。世界的に権威のある文学賞のひとつ。

Chapter 12: Structuralism

作家・（登場）人物・作品リスト

[William] Wordsworth：「ウィリアム・ワーズワース（1770-1850）」英国のロマン派詩人。『序曲』（*The Prelude*, 1805）は自伝的長篇詩。『逍遥』（*The Excursion*, 1815）は『隠者』（*The Recluse*）の一部となるはずだったが、後者は未完に終わった。

Henry James：「ヘンリー・ジェイムズ（1843-1916）」 ▶ Chapter 3 Narrative / Story

The Da Vinci Code：「『ダ・ヴィンチ・コード』（2003）」米国の作家ダン・ブラウン（Dan Brown, 1964- ）による長編小説。作中にルーヴル美術館が登場する。

[Adam] Dalgliesh：「アダム・ダルグリッシュ」英国の推理小説家Ｐ・Ｄ・ジェイムズ（P. D. James, 1920-2014）の人気小説シリーズの主人公。作者は 1991 年に「ホランド・パークのジェイムズ女男爵」（'Baroness James of Holland Park'）に叙された。

Sherlock Holmes：「シャーロック・ホームズ」英国の作家アーサー・コナン・ドイル（Arthur Conan Doyle, 1859-1930）の著作に登場する探偵。探偵の代名詞的存在。

Jonathan Culler：「ジョナサン・カラー（1944- ）」米国の文学批評家。構造主義をはじめとする文学理論の発展と普及に寄与した。

David Beckham：「デイヴィッド・ベッカム（1975- ）」英国の元サッカー選手。2000 年代に絶大な人気を誇った。利き足は左。

Roland Barthes：「ロラン・バルト（1915-80）」フランスの哲学者・批評家。「作者の死」（'La mort de l'auteur', 1967）や『テクストの快楽』（*Le Plaisir du texte*, 1973）などの著作で知られる。ステーキ・アンド・チップスに関するエッセイは『現代社会の神話』（*Mythologies*, 1957）に収められている。

Cinderella：「シンデレラ」 ▶ Chapter 3 Narrative / Story

Middlemarch：「『ミドルマーチ』（1871-72）」英国の作家ジョージ・エリオット（George Eliot, 1819-80）の代表作であり、イギリスの地方都市を舞台とした長編大作。初めは全 8 部が順々に出版され同時期に 4 巻本にまとめられたが、ペンギン・クラシックス版では一冊に収められている。 ▶ Chapter 4 Epic

[Salvador] Dali：「サルバドール・ダリ（1904-89）」スペインのシュルレアリスム画家。歪んだ時計は代表作「記憶の固執」（'La persistència de la memòria', 1931）に描かれている。

解説

imagistic：イマジズム（Imagism）は 20 世紀初頭に英米で起こった詩の運動。明確なイメージの提示によって現実を切り取ろうとしたイマジストたちは、しばしば極端に短い詩を書いた。運動自体は短命に終わったが、20 世紀文学に大きな影響を与えた。代表的な詩人に、エズラ・パウンド（Ezra Pound, 1885-1972）、ヒルダ・ドゥーリトル（Hilda Doolittle [H. D.], 1886-1961）らがいる。

Eureka!：古代ギリシア語で「見つけた！」を意味するこの語は、アルキメデス（Archimedes, 287-

212BC 頃）が物体の体積を量る方法を発見した際に発したとされている。その故事にちなんで、新たな発見やアイディア創造の喜びを表す言葉となった。

totemism：トーテム（totem）は特定の部族や親族などの社会集団を象徴する動植物。トーテム崇拝などを構造的な視点から研究したフランスの社会人類学者クロード・レヴィ＝ストロース（Claude Lévi-Strauss, 1908–2009）は、構造主義の祖とされる。

a beefsteak is a beefsteak is a beefsteak：米国の作家ガートルード・スタイン（Gertrude Stein, 1874–1946）の有名な言葉、'A rose is a rose is a rose'を踏まえた表現。「バラはバラでありそれ以外の何物でもない」という意味で解されることが多い。

Chapter 13: Deconstruction

作家・（登場）人物・作品リスト

Jacques Derrida：「ジャック・デリダ（1930–2004）」フランスの哲学者。「脱構築」、「差延」などの概念を創り出したことで知られる。著作に『グラマトロジーについて』（*De la grammatologie,* 1967）など。

Roland Barthes：「ロラン・バルト（1915–80）」 ▶ Chapter 12 Structuralism

Jacques Lacan：「ジャック・ラカン（1901–81）」フランスの精神分析家・精神科医。著作に『エクリ』（*Écrits,* 1966）など。

David Lodge：「デイヴィッド・ロッジ（1935- ）」英国の作家・英文学者。モリス・ザップ（Morris Zapp）が登場する『小さな世界』（*Small World,* 1984）は大学を舞台としたコミカルな小説。

Penelope：「ペーネロペー」ギリシア神話に登場する女性。オデュッセウスの妻。夫の長期不在の間、言い寄ってくる求婚者たちから逃れるため、「（夫のではなく）舅の死装束が完成したら結婚相手を選ぶ」と約束したうえで、昼に織った織物を夜になると解いていた。

Hamlet：『ハムレット』 ▶ Chapter 2 Ambiguity

Paul de Man：「ポール・ド・マン（1919–83）」米国の文学理論家。イェール学派の中心人物とみなされた。著書に『盲目と洞察』（*Blindness and Insight,* 1971）など。

All in the Family：『オール・イン・ザ・ファミリー』（1971-79）」アメリカで放映されたホームコメディー。

Till Death Do Us Part：『死が二人を分かつまで』（1965-75）」イギリスで放映されたホームコメディー。

W. B. Yeats：「W・B・イェイツ（1865–1939）」アイルランドの詩人・劇作家。1923 年度ノーベル文学賞受賞者。「学童の中で」（'Among the School Children'）は 1926 年に書かれた詩。

Ortwin de Graef：「オルトウィン・ド・グラーフ（1963- ）」ベルギーの文学研究者。博士課程の学生だった時に発見したポール・ド・マンの戦時中の記事は大きな波紋を広げた。

解説

theory：英米の学界において、20 世紀後半の西洋哲学に影響を受けた批評理論はまとめて 'theory' と呼ばれた。

inherently indeterminate：言語やテクストは「内的に決定不可能」、すなわちそもそもの性質として意味を決定できないということ。

écriture：「エクリチュール」は「書かれたもの、書くこと」を意味するフランス語。デリダは「語られたもの」に優位を与える西洋哲学の音声中心主義を批判するためにエクリチュールに着目した。

Oedipal intellectual mayhem：「エディプス的な知的騒乱」若手研究者による脱構築受容の動機を年長の研究者への対抗心に見る著者は、息子の父親への対抗心を分析したフロイトの理論「エディプス・コンプレックス」（▶ Chapter 2 Ambiguity）にそれをなぞらえる。

Strum und Drang：「疾風怒濤」18 世紀後半のドイツの文学運動。ゲーテ（Goethe ▶ Chapter 6 Culture）、シラー（Friedrich Schiller, 1759–1805）らの若い作家を中心として文学の革新が目指された。

Chapter 14: New Historicism

作家・(登場) 人物・作品リスト

Moby-Dick:『白鯨』(1851) ▶ Chapter 8 The Canon

John Webster:「ジョン・ウェブスター (1580–1632 など諸説あり)」エリザベス朝からジェームズ朝期イギリスの劇作家。『白い悪魔』(*The White Devil*, 1608 頃) や『モルフィ公爵夫人』(*The Duchess of Malfi*, 1614 頃) で知られる。

Thomas Middleton:「トマス・ミドルトン (1580–1627)」ジャコビアン時代のイングランドの劇作家。喜劇、悲劇の双方を手がけ、多作家で知られた。

[William] Shakespeare:「ウィリアム・シェイクスピア (1564–1616)」 ▶ Chapter 2 Ambiguity

Hamlet:「ハムレット」 ▶ Chapter 2 Ambiguity

Ophelia:「オフィーリア」『ハムレット』に登場するハムレットの妃候補。ハムレットに「尼寺に行け」('get thee to a nunnery') と命じられた末に、狂気に陥り溺死する。

Edward Alleyn:「エドワード・アレン (1566–1626)」エリザベス朝時代の有名俳優。売春宿を経営して一財を築いたとの通説がある。

Stephen Greenblatt:「スティーヴン・グリーンブラット (1943–)」新歴史主義の創始者と言われる米国の文学批評家、シェイクスピア研究者。

The Tempest:「『テンペスト』(1612)」シェイクスピア最後の戯曲。新歴史主義以降は帝国主義、植民地主義の観点から読まれることが増え、島に住む怪物キャリバン (Caliban) が植民地の被支配者の象徴として解釈されるようになった。

Frantz Fanon:「フランツ・ファノン (1925–61)」旧フランス植民地マルティニーク出身の思想家、革命家。アルジェリア革命に大きく貢献したほか、ポストコロニアル理論の先駆者とも言われる。著書に『地に呪われたる者』(*The Wretched of the Earth*, 1961) など。

négritude:「ネグリチュード」マルティニーク出身の詩人・評論家エメ・セゼール (Aimé Césaire, 1913–2008) らによって 1930 年代に創始された、黒人のアイデンティティを追求する思潮・文学運動。

[Jean-Jacques] Rousseau:「ジャン・ジャック・ルソー (1712–78)」フランスの哲学者、政治思想家。著書に『社会契約論』(*Du contrat social, ou principes du droit politique*, 1762)、『エミール』(*Émile, ou De l'éducation*, 1762) など。アウトサイダーや他者を意味する「高貴な野蛮人」(noble savage) の語を初めて用いたとされることがあるが、これは事実ではない。

[Karl] Marx:「カール・マルクス (1818–83)」 ▶ Chapter 7 Base / Superstructure

Clifford Geertz:「クリフォード・ギアツ (1926–2006)」アメリカの文化人類学者。バリ島をフィールドに数々の調査を行なったほか、解釈学派の人類学者として後世に多大な影響を与える。

解説

synchronic/diachronic：「共時的／通時的」スイスの言語学者ソシュール（Ferdinand de Saussure, 1857−1913）の用語。「共時的」は、時間の流れや歴史的変化を考慮せず記述するさまを指し、「通時的」は逆にそれらを考慮して記述するさまを指す。

Jacobean tragedy：「ジャコビアン時代の悲劇」そのモチーフからしばしば「復讐悲劇」と呼ばれ、ジェームズ1世時代（1603−25）に人気を博した演劇作品群。

textuality：「テクスト性」非言語的なものも含め、何であれ伝達可能な内容を持つものを分析可能な「テクスト」とみなす批評的態度。構造主義、ポスト構造主義の文学批評において顕著に現れた。

liminality：「リミナリティ」元は人類学の用語で、日常生活の規範から逸脱し、境界領域にある不安定な状態を指す。

【補足】ミシェル・フーコー（Michel Foucault, 1926-84）の諸概念、たとえばエピステーメー（ある時代の社会や人々が生産する知識のあり方を特徴づける知の枠組みを意味する）や知と権力（強制されるのではなく、知識として日常に浸透することで働く権力のあり方）などは、新歴史主義の発展に影響を与えたとされる。フーコーは1980年代にカリフォルニア大学バークリー校で教鞭を執っており、その時期にアメリカのアカデミアに新歴史主義が根を下ろしたという見方もできるだろう。

Chapter 15: Sexual Politics

作家・（登場）人物・作品リスト

Kate Millett：「ケイト・ミレット（1934–2017）」米国のフェミニスト活動家。著作『性の政治学』（*Sexual Politics*, 1970）で知られる。

Henry Miller：「ヘンリー・ミラー（1891–1980）」米国の作家で自伝的小説の『北回帰線』（*Tropic of Cancer*, 1934）や『セクサス』（*Sexus*, 1949）が有名。

Lady Chatterley：「『チャタレイ夫人』」英国作家 D・H・ロレンス（D. H. Lawrence, 1885–1930）の小説『チャタレイ夫人の恋人』（*Lady Chatterley's Lover*, 1928）のこと。1929 年に性的描写を削除した版で出版されていたが、1960 年の裁判の結果、無削除版が英国で出版された。

[Lucus] Cranach：「ルーカス・クラナッハ（1472–1553）」ドイツ・ルネサンスの代表的画家。宗教画・肖像画を描く一方で、女性の裸体画でも有名。彼の描くヴィーナスは裸体に帽子とネックレスをまとっているが故に、いっそうなまめかしい。

The Female Eunuch：「『去勢された女』（1970）」オーストラリア人のジャーメイン・グリア（Germaine Greer, 1939– ）の著作でフェミニズム運動に影響を与えた。

A Midsummer Night's Dream：「『真夏の夜の夢』（1594–95 頃）」シェイクスピアの喜劇。

Virginia Woolf：「ヴァージニア・ウルフ（1882–1941）」 ▶ Chapter 8 Canon

Betty Friedan：「ベティ・フリーダン（1921–2006）」米国のウーマンリブ運動（第二波フェミニズム）の主導者。著作『女らしさの神話』（*The Feminine Mystique*, 1963; 邦題『新しい女性の創造』）が有名。

Simone de Beauvoir：「シモーヌ・ド・ボーヴォワール（1908–86）」フランスの哲学者であり、フェミニズムの活動家。

Elaine Showalter：「エレイン・ショウォールター（1941– ）」米国の文学批評家・フェミニストで、著作に『女性自身の文学』（*A Literature of Their Own*, 1977）。

Sandra Gilbert and Susan Gubar：「サンドラ・ギルバート（1936– ）とスーザン・グーバー（1944– ）」いずれも米国の文学批評家・研究者で、『屋根裏の狂女』（*The Madwoman in the Attic*, 1979）を共著で出版。

Jane Eyre：「『ジェーン・エア』（1847）」シャーロット・ブロンテ（Charlotte Brontë, 1816–55）の小説。孤児として育った主人公ジェーンが地主ロチェスター家の家庭教師となり、主人と恋に落ち結婚することになるが、その直前、精神に異常を来した彼の妻（バーサ）の存在を知り……というのが前半のプロット。

[Geoffrey] Chaucer：「ジェフリー・チョーサー（1343 頃 –1400）」 ▶ Chapter 8 Canon

Anna Karenina：「アンナ・カレーニナ」 ▶ Chapter 1 Mimesis

Toni Morrison：「トニ・モリスン（1931–2019）」米国の作家・文学研究者。アフリカ系アメリカ人として初のノーベル文学賞を受賞。代表作に『青い眼がほしい』（*The Bluest Eye*, 1970）、『ビラヴド』

(*Beloved*, 1988)。

Joyce Carol Oates：「ジョイス・キャロル・オーツ（1938-）」米国の作家・文学研究者。

Gayatri Chakravorty Spivak：「ガヤトリ・C・スピヴァック（1942-）」インドのカルカッタ出身、米国の文学批評家でフェミニズム批評やポストコロニアル批評の論考を多数出版。

解説

the 'Years of the Young Rebels'：英国の詩人・小説家・批評家スティーヴン・スペンダー（Stephen Spender, 1909-95）の著作『若き叛逆者たちの年』（*The Year of the Young Rebels*, 1969）を踏まえた表現。

suttee：「サティー」ヒンドゥー教の習慣で、夫が死亡した際に、貞淑さの証明として寡婦が生きたまま焼かれる（強要されて焼身自殺を行なう）儀式。

gynocriticism：「ガイノクリティシズム」ショウォールターの造語で、文学的伝統における女性作家の系譜研究を指す。

three phases: feminine/feminist/female：3段階とは、「女性作家たちが支配的な男性の芸術的規範と美的基準を模倣した女性的段階（1840-80年）、次に急進的でしばしば分離主義の立場が主張されるフェミニズムの段階（1880-1920年）、そして最終的に、とりわけ女性の著作と経験とに注意を向けた女の段階（1920年以降）」（ピーター・バリー『文学理論講義』高橋和久監訳、141頁）を指す。

post-Freudian insight：父親の影響を重視し、母親の影響を軽視するフロイト的精神分析に修正を加えたフロイトの女性後継者たち、例えば、フロイトの娘のアンナ・フロイト（Anna Freud, 1895-1982）やメラニー・クライン（Melanie Klein, 1882-1960）などの成果を指す。

the literary machine：スピヴァックの1993年の著書のタイトル *Outside in the Teaching Machine* を踏まえた言い方。'Teaching Machine' は大学組織の中枢、とりわけカリキュラムの決定権がある教授陣を伝統的に男性が占めてきたことを暗示している。

50 LITERATURE IDEAS YOU REALLY NEED TO KNOW by John Sutherland
Copyright © John Sutherland 2010
Reproduced by permission of Quercus Editions Limited.

Literature Ideas You Really Need to Know:

From "Mimesis" to "Sexual Politics"

文学概念入門：〈ミメーシス〉から〈セクシュアル・ポリティクス〉まで

2021 年 4 月 10 日　　初版第 1 刷発行

著　者　John Sutherland
編著者　宮本 文／桐山大介／小島尚人／千代田夏夫／ハーン小路恭子

発行者　森　信久
発行所　**株式会社　松 柏 社**
〒 102-0072　東京都千代田区飯田橋 1-6-1
TEL　03 (3230) 4813（代表）
FAX　03 (3230) 4857
http://www.shohakusha.com
e-mail: info@shohakusha.com

英文校閲　　Howard Colefield
装　　幀　　小島トシノブ（NONdesign）
印刷・製本　シナノ書籍印刷株式会社

ISBN978-4-88198-769-8
略号 = 769